ANTHARJANAM

ANTHARJANAM

MEMOIRS OF A NAMBOODIRI WOMAN

Devaki Nilayamgode

Translated from Malayalam by
Indira Menon and Radhika P. Menon

With an Introduction by
J. Devika

Illustrations by
Namboodiri

OXFORD
UNIVERSITY PRESS

OXFORD
UNIVERSITY PRESS

Oxford University Press is a department of the University of Oxford.
It furthers the University's objective of excellence in research, scholarship,
and education by publishing worldwide. Oxford is a registered trademark of
Oxford University Press in the UK and in certain other countries

Published in India
by Oxford University Press
YMCA Library Building, Jai Singh Road, New Delhi 110 001, India

ISBN-13: 978-0-19-807416-8
ISBN-10: 0-19-807416-6

Typeset in 11/13 Garamond Premier Pro
By Excellent Laser Typesetters, Pitampura, Delhi 110 034
Printed in India at Artxel, New Delhi 110 020

MR. Omayal Achi MR. Arunachalam Trust was set up in 1976 to further education
and health care particularly in rural areas. The MR. AR Educational Society was later
established by the Trust. One of the Society's activities is to sponsor Indian literature.
This translation is entirely funded by the MR. AR Educational Society as part of it aims.

Contents

Author's Note

In 2003, just after my seventy-fifth birthday, I published a slim book of my memoirs (*Nashtabodhangalillathe*) which literally means 'with no sense of loss or regret'. Until then, I had never thought I could write at all. I began to do so because of the persistent entreaties and persuasion of my grandson, Tathagatan, who during his early college days, stayed with me in Thrissur.

The book was about growing up in the loveless, dim environs of a Namboodiri household in central Kerala, even as the winds of change began to sweep over the community in the 1930s and 1940s. The Malayalam-reading public responded enthusiastically to my recollections, which, in turn, encouraged me to continue recalling them. Three years later, I published *Yaathra: Kaattilum, Naattilum* which literally means 'a journey through lands and forests', reaching deeper and further back into my own social and personal history. Friendly editors of Malayalam periodicals K.C. Narayanan, Kamal Ram Sajeev, and O.K. Johnny, and publishing houses readily indulged me. As a result, I now have four books in print.

I often see announcements about the youngest writers and youngest poets. Well! I must have set some sort of record for beginning to write so late in life.

This volume is a collection of writings selected from my above-mentioned books and some articles published at random in different Malayalam periodicals. Radhika P. Menon worked on *Nashtabodhan-galillathe* and Indira Menon on *Yaathra: Kaattilum, Naattilum* and the stand-alone articles. Nevertheless, the book is presented so brilliantly that it now has a chronological and thematic structure—almost linear, with a seemingly uninterrupted narrative running through it—thanks to the high discerning faculty of the book's editor, Mini Krishnan of Oxford University Press. It is my greatest fortune that my writings drew her attention, and that OUP decided to bring out an English version of my selected writings.

My unbounded gratitude to Radhika P. Menon and Indira Menon for their excellent translations. I am indebted to J. Devika for her learned introduction which has provided my memoirs with their essential historical background. I also wish to thank Namboodiri for his drawings which add immense narrative value to my text.

DEVAKI NILAYAMGODE

May 2011

Translators' Notes

While the pleasures of translating this narrative are, I hope, evident in the translation itself, I shall confine myself here to the challenges of translation posed by Devaki Nilayamgode's *Yaathra*. Since I wish to keep my comments specific to this text, I shall not even attempt to deal with the many complex and formidable problems that a translator usually encounters. The cultural differences between the host and the target languages have long been discussed. The nuances of phrases, especially when a dialect is involved, pose an almost insurmountable difficulty. All these could be addressed to an extent, however inadequately, by the use of footnotes or the glossary. But the debate between the usefulness of the one against the other continues unabated. All these and more—including the gendered question of whether translation is subservient to the text—are hotly stated and contested.

Without opening up any of these arguments, however, I want to talk about the language and emotions of *this* text. Even though she chronicles a life of deprivation, lived with great hardship, Nilayamgode has chosen not to be judgemental about the people and events in her life. There is no discernible anger at the unfairness of the treatment of women, and of herself in particular. If there are questions, then they are stated quietly and not with virulence or vituperation. Her demands are also made gently and not with any stridency. But underneath the calm surface there is a lurking whirlpool ready to suck her in if she allows it. This deceptive manner can allow a reader to see only the writer's acquiescence to cruelty, and not the questions swirling between and beyond the words. Readers who occupy different cultural spaces may not have much sympathy for such acceptance when it is all they can see. The different ways in which various people react to emotional turbulence create a hurdle in transcreating anger, pain, joy, or love in a foreign language. This was the major problem I faced while translating the text.

On the surface, Nilayamgode's prose is placid and calm. The translator's job, then, is to bring out the steely quality behind the apparent pliancy: the strength that any woman or girl in her situation must possess in order to retain her sanity. Of course the seeming acceptance becomes less difficult for her because of her upbringing. But beyond such acquiescence is a thinking, probing, questioning, intelligent mind which rejects the false values of society. It is this mind that needs to be brought to the fore in a translation, alongside the apparent placidity of its acceptance of circumstances.

Like nature on which she dwells in such detail, Nilayamgode's character descriptions, too, are gentle and violent in turn. Both nurture and destroy. But the very fact that they do both is testimony to the fact that there is hope for her people. Women like her suffer—yes, more in her community than in others—but somehow there is also a universalism to their predicament that makes *Yaathra* more than an account of this particular *antharjanam*. Her suffering crosses cultural spaces to speak to a wide audience. However, in order to allow her voice to be fully heard, I had to find a way to tease out the nuances of the words and their contexts. Often, this was an uphill task.

In many ways, my difficulty stemmed from Nilayamgode's language, itself, which is simple, unadorned, and stark to the point of being bare. While such starkness works in the host language, the translator has to do more than record the facts and translate the comments. She also has to convey nuances. But where there is such spare language, there is minimal scope for expansion, and I had to keep close to the text. This close adherence to the host text, however, can affect the felicity that is essential to appreciating the unspoken layers of Nilayamgode's narrative. At times, it can even lead the reader to lose sight of the creativity that is essential to appreciating a work of art.

Most of all, while working with minimal language, one has to find a way of bringing emotional upheavals to the surface without making them obtrusive. The deceptive surface that I have already mentioned must be maintained while making apparent the emotional struggles beneath it. This is a difficult task when the text does not allow you to speak openly about the struggles. The semiotics of one language and culture differs from another, rendering some signs not easily comprehensible in the target language. Sometimes these signs can even look downright ridiculous. However, there is also a universalism that translates easily between cultural and linguistic contexts. The translator, thus, has to walk the thin line between close adherence and transcreation, which may leave her open to the criticism of having departed from the text. These are some of the risks I have had to face while translating Nilayamgode's story. But these traversals are crucial to the very title of the narrative—*Yaathra*—which means, of course, a journey, a travelling between places that bear the marks of all ports of call. In what follows, I hope these marks are visible only to render more vibrant the emotional complexity of Nilayamgode's narrative. The journey you are about to undertake is a journey the text has already undergone.

This journey could not have been undertaken without the active support of Mini Krishnan, the editor. She walked with me every step of the way, guiding, advising, making my passage less difficult. The final version would not have read as it does without her active participation. Her input and suggestions added to the quality of the translation. I am grateful to her for her help. I'm also grateful to Lekshmy Rajeev who, on Mini's request, translated the verses of *Sheelavati* at short notice. Her translation of these songs is evocative of their spirit which could not have been achieved without her help. I also acknowledge the vigorous partnership I enjoyed with my co-translator P. Radhika whom I have not had the good fortune of meeting. Last but most of all, I thank the author herself, Devaki Nilayamgode.

INDIRA MENON

May 2011

More often than not, there is a host of personal reasons behind an act of literary translation. The most basic among them is that when a text strikes a chord in a reader's heart, the natural impulse is to share it with a larger community that may derive equal pleasure out of it. And if the same text offers strong academic reasons, too, for its translation, the enterprise becomes doubly gratifying. Devaki Nilayamgode's memoir in Malayalam *Nashtabodhangalillathe* was a work that lingered in my mind long after it was put away and almost seemed to demand entry into a world beyond the Malayalam-reading one. The reasons for this fascination are many. First and most important, it gives a brief glimpse of a lost culture and helps correct several myths that surround it.

'*Antharjanams*' have always been a source of great fascination in popular imagination in Kerala. To an outsider's eyes, they were living exotica. Cocooned in luxury, shielded from public view, always escorted by an entourage of obsequious attendants and endlessly enjoying a hedonistic life full of festivals and elaborate feasts, these upper-caste women appeared to lead a charmed existence. However, what most people never realized was that the antharjanams' awe-inspiring exclusivity concealed the cruellest form of patriarchal oppression that robbed them not only of independence and education but even the simplest and most innocent of joys. Nilayamgode's autobiographical writing focuses on the penumbral region between the intensely private and the totally public—a space which outsiders have preferred to paint in flatteringly unrealistic colours—and attempts to restore it to less flamboyant but more realistic tones. It honestly sketches some of the beliefs, practices, and rituals of the Namboodiris that made life within their closed system insufferable for women.

However, *Nashtabodhangalillathe* is not merely about the problems that afflicted that community. Its canvas accommodates many positive sketches as well, the most significant among them being the incipient stages of the reform movement which brought about radical changes in the structure of the Namboodiri family and the power equations that operated within it. Within this larger picture there are very personal mini-narratives that project impressive as well as touching images of small acts of resistance within Nilayamgode's natal family—ranging from covert attempts at circumventing age-old taboos to very bold acts of breaking life-sapping, reactionary conventions. The girls of Pakaravoor *illam* seeking the help of their maids in order to secretly read books during periods of menstruation, their brothers defying tradition by joining members of other castes in feasts, and similar deeds are instances which testify to their inherent and irrepressible sense of intellectual curiosity as well as their robust social sense. Indirectly, they also show how the ambience in each Namboodiri home was naturally and inevitably veering towards a more organized reformation struggle that would change the culture and lifestyle of a community forever.

Its truth value and historical importance apart, *Nashtabodhangal-illathe* reveals the inner beauty of the person who authored it. Despite serious setbacks (being deprived of formal education being the most crucial among them) Nilayamgode betrays no sense of bitterness or righteous indignation. This tonal balance informs the entire narrative and gives it a certain depth that would be inconceivable if she had adopted any specific ideological perspective or a rigid stance. Her ambiguous-sounding comments on the infamous trial of Kuriyedathu Thaatri are a superb example of her essential humanism:

Thaatri, who had slept with prominent Vedic teachers of the community, famous artistes and powerful men, had preserved a meticulous record of the date, zodiac sign and day of her liaison with each of them. It seems she had even jotted down, in palm leaf documents, details about their birthmarks. Had she foreseen that these bits of information would one day come to her rescue and provide valuable evidence?

There is no trace of moral judgement in these lines—no condemnation either of Thaatri or of her numerous paramours or of the jurors, no hectoring about the injustices within the social norms of the times, no exploration into the factors that precipitated the crisis, no inflamed feminist rhetoric, not an iota of pornographic detail—in fact, the description is almost deadpan and bland. At first sight, the chapter on Kuriyedathu Thaatri seems to have ignored a rich mine of sociological analysis and missed an opportunity to launch on a personal commentary. However, the reader is not likely to experience any sense of loss at this authorial reticence. The question that Nilayamgode gently inserts at the end of the passage reveals her thoroughly honourable intention—she merely seeks a non-judgemental yet sympathetic response towards a woman who was richly endowed but whose life inexplicably and sadly went askew.

Nilayamgode maintains this tone of detachment throughout the work. But the reader is never bored because the narration is occasionally relieved by touches of gentle humour. And, invariably, she herself is the target of the soft barbs. For instance, the description of little Devaki adding Victor Hugo's Bishop of D. to the pantheon of Hindu gods in her puja room or of her memorizing the laudatory verses of K.P. Namboodiri's tooth powder even while keeping her personal stock of the product untouched, brings a kindly smile to reader's lips.

It is noteworthy that even in the handling of more serious matters, she moves on an even emotional keel. When she mentions how she escaped the rigours of orthodoxy through a fortuitous marriage and savoured moderate success by participating in a reformation struggle later on, she does not crow with delight or shout triumphantly. The memoir paints no heroes or villains; and, precisely for that reason, there are no effusive descriptions, either admiring or vitriolic. With an almost unconscious use of understatement, her story thus leaves behind an enduring image of a community that was cruel in its own way but was not without a share of genuine goodness, beauty, and charity.

Ironically, it was this very quality of dignified restraint that posed the greatest challenge in the process of translation. So deep and pervasive is the gentleness of her perspective that it is hard to find even a single sentence in the entire narrative that either sounds bold or reads like an assertion. While this by itself creates no particular problem to the translator, a loyal translation can nevertheless be a stumbling block to the readers of its English version and deny them a peek into the subtle historical or cultural nuances of certain seemingly mundane observations that Malayalis, conversant with the social movements of the state, can access without any difficulty.

For instance, the brief description of Nilayamgode's mother in the Malayalam text comes through as a neutral statement of fact. An exact rendering would be: 'Amma could read the Puranas. Generally, girls were not given education'. To a Malayali who knows about the true extent of orthodoxy and female illiteracy that prevailed in Kerala even during the late nineteenth century, these two sentences, their apparent disconnect-edness, and plainness notwithstanding, can very powerfully convey how unusual the lady's accomplishment was. However, if the translator chooses to remain true to the muted style of the original text, he/she runs the risk of muffling the potency of the detail. Hence, the choice of a slightly more emphatic version: 'At a time when girls were barely educated, Amma could read the *Puranas*'. In the process, the tone of detachment that characterizes the original has given way to one of superiority and the bare description has morphed into a mild claim. Such a distortion is perhaps condonable because the shift in tenor brings with it the compensatory benefit of foregrounding a piece of sociologically important information that would otherwise escape the notice of the English-reading public.

Another issue that required considerable thought was whether to retain certain loaded native terms or to use their rough English equivalents. The latter choice had the obvious advantage of instant connect with the reader but ran the risk of obscuring the finer cultural details contained in them. The word '*irrikanammamar*' was one such word. When the first translated version of Nilayamgode's narrative appeared in print in *Samyukta* (a journal of women's studies published from Thiruvananthapuram), I had changed it into 'women attendants'. In the subsequent series of revisions, however, I preferred to keep the native term in order to preserve its rich meaning as well as local flavour. The same logic decided the use of '*amma*' and '*achan*' in preference to 'mother' and 'father'; the choice of '*pathayappura*' over 'barn house', '*oottuppura*' over 'dining hall', and so on.

But certain other native words would not permit deferment of their explanatory notes to the glossary. In such cases, though very rarely in this text, I had to take a bit of liberty and bring the meaning into the text. The appending of the phrase 'literally meaning "object" as the erring antharjanam was called' to the word '*saadhanam*' was necessary lest the non-Malayali reader should overlook the heavy patriarchal bias embedded in the trial of Kuriyedathu Thaatri.

The decision to go for such alterations was often very difficult to take and on such occasions Mini Krishnan's expert editorial advice was immensely crucial. In fact, she has played a very significant role in nudging the translation through several drafts, removing the dross that stuck to its first versions, and refining the product till it shone. Words are inadequate to express my gratitude to her and to three friends—G.S. Jayasree, Sreedevi K. Nair, and Jayasree Ramakrishnan Nair—who were staunch pillars of support all through the process.

RADHIKA P. MENON

May 2011

Introduction
The Namboodiris of Kerala

THE PAST IS A FOREIGN LAND

Never has my heart shuddered harder than when I placed my hand in the gap of that door—that door, which was thought to be impregnable, stronger than an iron fortress ... A bit of pride and irrepressible optimism were all that I had. Both were illusory. What had I achieved, to be proud? It was not just my hands that had brought down that obsolete decaying door. It was broken down by the sighs that had smouldered within for many centuries; it collapsed from the force of many, many women breaking their heads against it. However, what had actually been gained by simply breaking down just this door? How many doors would we have to break down in order to reach that world of security and love that we longed for?

Thus mused Lalitambika Antharjanam, one of the greatest heroines of reformism in Kerala and of Malayala Brahmin community reformism in particular, on the challenges that modern educated women of her community faced in the early half of the twentieth century. By 1969, when this autobiographical piece had appeared in print, the traditional world of Kerala's Brahmins—or the Namboodiris, as they are often referred to— had receded considerably. Memories of that world could never be neutral, for they were most often penned by people whose sweat and tears had blended into the project of breaking out of traditional life into what they thought was the freedom of the modern world. In the alluring light of the emotional warmth and closeness that modern conjugality and domesticity seemed to promise, the grim unsentimental iron-rule of hierarchy within the traditional domestic space of the Malayala Brahmin homestead, the *illam*, appeared contrary to natural instinct and culturally abhorrent as well. Strikingly, much of these recollections stress not only the sheer oppressiveness of everyday life within the traditional Namboodiri community but also the strangeness of it all. And this was being pointed out by reformers as early as the 1930s. Lalitambika Antharjanam ended her powerful short story *Vidhibalam* ('The Strength of Fate') written in the 1930s that depicted the last meeting between an aged Malayala Brahmin woman—an *antharjanam* ('the indoor people', literally)—who had been ostracized and had later married a Muslim, and her son, separated from her as a child, sighing eloquently: 'Penance for seeing one's own mother! God! The customs of some communities!'

Seventy years later, after the twentieth century had ended, comes a voice from the same past with similar musings on the strangeness of it all, in the memories of Devaki Nilayamgode.

This sense of strangeness was, in a sense, the culmination of a flood-tide of change that the Namboodiri community experienced in the twentieth century. The role of radical community reformism, beginning in the early twentieth century through the Namboodiri Yoga Kshema Sabha (YKS from now), in bringing about this change has been widely acknowledged. This organization sought to recreate the community to meet the challenges of the times, and to bring all the sub-groups within the community together to shape a modern community.

SOURCES OF POWER

The Namboodiris' dominant position in Malayalee society of the early twentieth century was firmly rooted in a long history of political and cultural authority and material dominance, strong enough to have survived the powerful monarchies of eighteenth century Kerala, Tipu Sultan's invasion of Malabar, and British rule. The two sources of their power—they were the landowning aristocracy as well as the religious elite—were well-knit enough in the early twentieth century to be designated 'theocratic feudalism' by the eminent anthropologist A. Aiyappan. While the

'Namboodiris' included more and less powerful groups, they certainly commanded greater resources than any other section of traditional society. They exercised significant control over land—the *Brahmaswam* and *Devaswam* lands granted to Brahmins and temples respectively, until the twentieth century. Their influence was greatest in the fertile river-valley zones, to which they are believed to have migrated between the third and eighth centuries. Origin myths such as in the *Keralolppatti* and *Keralamahatmyam* claim that the warrior-sage Parashurama settled them as masters of the land in sixty-four Brahmin villages in Tulunad and Kerala as *Bhudevas*, earthly gods, who were to be served by all others. They claimed that the Sudra women of Kerala, mainly of the temple castes and the Nairs, were descended from heavenly *Apsaras* and, as the descendants of these divine women of pleasure, were duty-bound to give pleasure to the *Bhudevas*.

This eminence was bolstered by an elaborate, sophisticated set of social arrangements that preserved the exclusivity and authority of the Namboodiris and simultaneously allowed them to maintain different balances of distance and closeness with different groups, extracting different sorts of material gain and services from each. These were the *Anaacharams*—observances unique to Malayala Brahmins, sanctioned by a text attributed to Sankara, the *Sankarasmriti*, which set them apart from Brahmins elsewhere. Thus in the *illams* that housed large Malayala Brahmin patrilineal joint families, everyday life was inconceivable without the services of the Nair *adiyar* (the servant-class) as ayahs, sweepers, maid-cum-companions, managers, male domestic helpers, guards, and so on. Strict rules, however, were laid down which regulated interaction between family members and other Brahmin visitors or guests with the Nair servant class. As for the castes lower down, inflexible and complicated rules of untouchability and unapproachability preserved the exclusivity of Malayala Brahmins. Lower caste people who breached the rules of unapproachability could be killed without a trial, much to the consternation of the missionaries who worked in Malayalee society in the nineteenth century. The Malayala Brahmins were themselves organized as several separate groups or sub-castes, linked to each other by strict rules of hierarchy and appropriate conduct: for instance, while both the *Aaddhyan* and the *Aasyan* sub-castes were counted as 'Namboodiri', the superiority of the former within the larger group was clearly institutionalized in norms and practices. Such a complicated system of layers and hierarchies served to manage a great deal of *internal* diversity and inequality—'Namboodiris' ranged from royal families such as those of the rajas of Edappally and Chempakaserry, to impoverished temple priests; from families that practiced 'good' magic to others that pursued the black arts and worshipped non-Aryan deities and serpents. There was even a matrilineal family, the *Ammomanmar* of Tazhakkat. There were Namboodiri families that practised medicine; the eight prominent Namboodiri families that specialized in medicine continue to be prominent, referred to as the *Ashtavaidyans*. Thus, the figure of the healer of snake-venom that Nilayamgode sketches in her memoirs was by no means an isolated one; on the contrary, such figures were fully integrated into the complicated internal hierarchy of the traditional Namboodiri community.

SAMBANDHAM: INTIMACY-IN-DISTANCE

The feature mentioned earlier—that of the achievement of intimacy-in-distance through an elaborate set of rules and arrangements undergirding the social and economic power of the Malayala Brahmins—was best illustrated in the institution of *sambandham*. The system of primogeniture prevalent among them was such that only the eldest son could marry from his own caste. Younger males were to seek alliances with women of the matrilineal castes, which included the Kshatriya, the Nair groups, and the temple castes, who often had considerable access to culture, learning, and the new currents emerging in early twentieth century Malayalee society. Children of such unions were members of their mother's families, with no formal claims upon their father's; interaction between partners was subject to strict regulation of time (hour, frequency, duration of visits by the man to the woman's home and vice-versa), space (either visiting Nair wives at their homes, or maintaining them in spaces set apart in the illam), exchange and conduct (of permissible gifts, obligations, dress, demeanour). These alliances were referred to by the neutral term sambandham that meant, simply and literally, 'alliance' or 'connection'.

Sambandham was loudly denounced in the radical wave of reformism within the Namboodiri reform movement of the 1930s. It was condemned for having allegedly promoted irresponsibility, licentiousness, and laziness among younger male members, for adding to the misery of antharjanams as the number of bridegrooms were limited, and for being 'against nature', and 'culturally and morally inferior'. At the annual conference of the YKS in 1929, the liberals named the entrance and exits of the venue *Vivahasanmargam* (The Virtuous Path of Marriage) and *Sambandhadurmargam* (Evil Path of *Sambandham*) respectively, which left the conservative members fuming.

Yet, to many antharjanams, the sight of the strikingly different Nair women and their children linked to the illam was the first glimpse of the 'freedom' and 'pleasures' of the 'world outside', as Nilayamgode's own account testifies. Nair sophistication, both of body and mind, served to highlight the grim, grey life of Brahmin women. Reformers were keen to point out that the antharjanam's misery was not just limited to the monotony and ritualism of their everyday lives: the Namboodiri husband in real life often exercised the power to send an erring wife to her grave. The prominent Namboodiri reformer M.R. Bhattatiripad's explosive play *Marakkudaikkullile Mahanarakam* (The Hell beneath the Cadjan Umbrella) which dwelt upon the violence inflicted by a husband upon his wife, it is claimed, was based upon a true incident.

LIFE AS AN ANTHARJANAM

Gender was undoubtedly one of the major axes of internal regulation among the Malayala Brahmins. All women (past puberty) had to observe elaborate seclusion (*ghosha*), and they moved out of their homes only with the cloak (*putappu*) and the large cadjan umbrella (*kuta*). Their domesticity was a highly ritualized one, combined with considerable amounts of domestic labour. The arduousness of domestic work within the illams was commented upon in the early twentieth century. An article which appeared in 1907 in the women's magazine *Lakshmibhayi*, signed 'KPM', lamented the taxing nature of the antharjanams' labour but also interpreted it as evidence for their strength and skill:

Look at the homesteads of the Namboodiris, who are esteemed for their wealth and noble birth. In many of these, which require one or two paras [a local measure of weight] of rice and adequate quantities of side dishes to go along with for a meal, the entire burden of the cooking is borne by two or three antharjanams all by themselves. What's more, even during feasting on occasions like the *Othootu*, [traditional recitation of the Vedas by Brahmins] these women gather some of their female relatives to prepare all the dishes quite effortlessly. Even *Valalan* [Bhima's disguise in the *Mahabharata,* as a skilled male cook] himself would bow in assent if he saw these moon-faced maidens lift up huge brass vessels brimming with hot cooked rice with their bangled, vine-like, delicate arms and coolly tilting them to drain off the rice-gruel, in full view of their heartless men. Simply compare the fare prepared by the traditional [male] Brahmin cooks of the *Agrasala* [temple kitchen] at Thiruvananthapuram, or the dishes cooked in the *Valiya Adukkala* ['big kitchen'] of the Vaikam temple, where the chief cook Muttassu Namboodiri and his assistants toil, sweaty, smoke-smothered, teary-eyed and forever blowing their noses, eight out of ten of which are unfit to be placed upon the tongue, with those cooked with nonchalant ease by these jewels of Womanliness—the comparison itself will be rendered superfluous.

The ritualized nature of this domesticity, which for Nilayamgode, formed the very stuff of everyday life in the illam of her childhood, was perceived as a serious impediment to the spread of modern education among the antharjanams. Responding to the queries of the Namboodiri Female Education Commission of 1927 instituted by the YKS, Madampu Narayanan Namboodiri remarked:

... they [antharjanams] start working in the kitchen by the age of eight ... when a few years pass in this fashion other tasks are loaded on ...what is called *Nedikkal* [making offerings] ... From early morning to 10 o'clock there is nothing but *nedikkal* and *namaskaram* towards east, towards south, what more, to every corner. To *Guruvayur Appan, Vaikkattappan, Kavil Shastavu* and every other deity ... Then the two Nazhikas [the Malayalee measure of time] in the afternoon are set apart to reading Puranas and *Charadu Pidichu Japikkal* [repeating holy chants a certain number of times everyday with one's fingers upon the thread worn around the neck] ...

In any case, to go out to school, antharjanams would have had to adopt modern ways of dressing, which was forbidden to them. Dress codes for both men and women in illams were strictly fixed according to custom, and signified caste position. As with everything else, even bedecking the body was subjugated to ritual purposes. In Namboodiri reformism, the issue of dress was a charged one, for both men and women. Women and men went bare-bodied, and those who wore shirts were instantly recognized as non-brahmin. This, however, changed in the course of the Namboodiri reform movement, more quickly for men. In the modern school established by reformers for Namboodiri boys at Edakkunni, initially there were strict rules disallowing teachers and students from wearing shirts during formal sessions. However, at the twenty-first session of the YKS, participants did not bathe, nor did they remove their shirts before lunch, which was regarded as revolutionary change. Reformers also advocated the abandonment of traditional dressing by antharjanams, warning them that if they did not do so, the popularization of intra-caste marriages, a major goal of Namboodiri reformism, would be difficult to attain, and that this would affect antharjanams adversely. In his famous address in 1931, V.T. Bhattatiripad openly voiced disgust at the lack of aesthetic dressing among the anthrajanams:

Many of us are turning head over heels about this [i.e. about intra-caste marriage] not because of our fascination for your sense of beauty, but merely out of a concern for morality. I do not hide the fact that many of us who are married are fed up of your ugly, disgusting dress and ornamentation, and are able to do no more than curse ourselves.

Many male reformers of the early twentieth century have remarked that a powerful if subtle network of reminders worked tirelessly to instil in women a sense of inferiority right from their infancy. Kanippayur Sankaran Nambudiripad, a prominent figure of the early twentieth century in his memoir *Ente Smaranakal* (1965) remembers that the submission of the female members was fostered in illams in many ways, like, for example, through preferential consideration towards boys from early infancy. Boys and girls were strictly segregated from an early age physically, and subject to very different daily routines. The obligations and bonds of marriage too were apparently quite different—indeed the nature of marriage in the traditional way of life was the target of some of the most severe criticism of the reformers. It was pointed out that the tie of marriage, called *Veli*, involved no bonds of emotional commitment, and was contracted merely for the sake of maintaining the ritualistic practices of the illam, for obtaining heirs, or worse, to facilitate the marriage of daughters. Ties between brothers and sisters, it was observed, did not involve an obligation on the former to assume responsibility for the latter, except to get them married, in the absence of older men who would have otherwise assumed it. The woman was totally amalgamated with her husband's family after marriage, and she used the same terms to address his relatives as he did. Polygamy was permitted to the eldest son, who alone was allowed to marry from his caste, as a male heir was indispensable. Widow remarriage was proscribed; indeed, the plight of young widows and antharjanams married off to men on their deathbeds (who, the reformers often pointed out, married these young girls sometimes to facilitate the marriages of their daughters!) was to be frequently evoked in defense of radical Namboodiri reformism. Marriage involved dowry payments. Women could not inherit land; so their dowry was given as moveable property. The heaviness of dowry payments was frequently mentioned in the early twentieth century discussions on the condition of the Malayala Brahmins in the nascent Malayalee public sphere.

Women who transgressed sexual norms were subjected to a ritualized 'trial', the *Smartavicharam*. T.K. Gopal Panikkar described the *Smarthavicharam* as it was practiced in Malabar in the early twentieth century, in his description of social life in Malabar, *Malabar and its Folk* (1900). It is evident from his account and many other contemporary accounts that this 'trial' was actually its exact opposite—an *anti-trial*—as the chief intention of the judges was not to provide the accused a chance to defend herself, but to extract a damning self-condemnation from her. *Smarthavicharam* proceedings began when the husband of the woman suspected of 'adulterous conduct' informed the local caste elder, who then communicated with the local chieftain who was considered the guardian of *mamool* or caste order. The rajahs of Cochin and Travancore, the Zamorin of Calicut, and other chieftains usually received such information and commissioned four caste elders (*vaidikans*) to hold 'trial'. The 'trial' was held in the woman's illam and involved considerable expense which could even ruin the family. Panikkar writes:

They then first hold what is called the *Dasivicharam*. The maid-servant attached to the house is first put up. She is worried by questions by the presiding judges; and if she consistently and openly denies the truth of the affair the inquiry naturally falls through for want of evidence. If, however, her evidence favours the allegation she is soon discharged and the Numbutiri woman concerned is made over to the *Anchampura* or a separate house and is thereafter cut off from all free movements in the family; and the whole family is likewise placed under a temporary social ban... The woman is then made to stand behind a curtain and is compelled to answer all the interrogatories put to her. She is subjected to a very rigorous and searching cross-examination until in the end she comes to admit her guilt. In the course of examination all sorts of stratagems are resorted to. Advice, entreaties, and threats are pressed into service. Even the nearest relatives of the woman, lest the taint might affect them also, strenuously aid in wringing the confession by their advice and entreaties. It may take days and months before the final confession is made. It is significant that nothing short of an actual confession of guilt will justify her removal from society. Anyhow sooner or later she makes her confession; and the judges then make a report about it to the social chieftain who, on receipt of the report, forthwith issues a proclamation banishing her from society and leaving her to take what course she would ...

From these accounts, the casting-out ceremony appears to have been equally painful. The woman's cadjan (umbrella), the symbol of her antharjanam-hood and her marriage-emblem, the *thaali-charadu*, would be ritually broken by a Nair servant. Her funeral ceremonies would then be performed. 'She is thereafter an outcaste woman with no community of social or religious, or domestic interest with her caste people', wrote Panikkar. The men she named as her accomplices were also outcast; however, if they were Namboodiris, they could obtain a *pampu* from a caste-elder, which would allow them to either perform penance, or prove their 'innocence' through specific 'trials' in temples like Suchindram and Guruvayoor. The woman, however, was cast out for good.

VICTIM OR SURVIVOR?

Does this mean that the antharjanam was meek, suffering, passive, the quintessential victim of patriarchy? The language of the early twentieth century Namboodiri reformers may lead one to think so. The best-beloved of all Namboodiri reformers of early twentieth century Kerala, V.T. Bhattatiripad, once remarked that the antharjanams resembled the discoloured bell-metal pots wasting away inside the lofts of the Namboodiri homesteads. The lack of agency implied through this reduction of the women to the instruments of their domestic labour echoed in the words of K. Devaki Antharjanam, who became a member of the Sree Mulam Legislative Assembly in the princely State of Travancore (south Kerala). In her speech in the Assembly in 1937, when the radical wing of Namboodiri social reformism had peaked, she remarked:

Most antharjanams observe ghosha [seclusion]. They have eyes but are prohibited from seeing anything pleasant. They have legs but their movement is circumscribed. Their state is quite like that of household utensils. ... In short the antharjanam is a jailed creature. Antharjanams are constantly watched; they are not permitted to breathe fresh air, to see the world. An antharjanam is born crying, lives her life in tears and dies weeping.

However, one must remain cautious about such accounts. There are hints, even in the accounts of the reformers themselves, that antharjanams were not entirely passive. Antharjanams, especially among the Malayala Brahmin aristocracy, often obtained some knowledge of the letters, with which they often read the sacred texts. A chapter in Nilayamgode's memoirs is devoted to memories of her erratic 'studying'. Pre-pubertal marriages were uncommon, not sanctioned by the *Anaachaarams* which the Malayala Brahmins had to adhere to. Gender difference was certainly important but was not the sole basis upon which this structure of regulation rested; considerations of age, position in the kin network and intra-caste hierarchy, marital status, and other factors were also crucial. The very structure of regulation itself permitted potentially subversive spaces. The antharjanams' extreme seclusion, the practice of their travelling without husbands escorted by servants, the extreme difficulties, material and otherwise, in conducting *Smarttavicharam*, all left spaces in which the rules ordering everyday life could be potentially upturned. To modern observers, the presence of such spaces indicated the 'decay' of the community. Indeed, in the early twentieth century, the *Malayala Manorama*, raised the alarm that the women and the servant-class in the illams were colluding against the men and that breaches of chastity were on the rise among antharjanams, and pleading that patriarchy among the Malayala Brahmins should be reinstated on more modern, stronger foundations. Accounts of reformers themselves reveal fault-lines that indicate not so much a total subordination of one sex by the other in the illam, but a more complex, mobile play of power with other factors like age, seniority, or 'moral authority' in very specific settings tilting the balance. V.T. Bhattatiripad's own story of the staging of his radical reformist play *Adukkalayil Ninnu Arangathekku* ('From the Kitchen to the Floodlit Stage') at his illam illustrates this complexity well. He relates how his orthodox older brother's opposition was overcome finally by the arguments of his aged grand-aunt, a widow.

No wonder, then, that the female protagonists of many of Lalitambika Antharjanam's scorching depictions of women's lives, under traditional Namboodiri domesticity, display many signs of being highly individuated. This is especially evident in their use of strategies to resist tradition—the young antharjanam of *Moodupadattil* ('Within the Veil') (1940) struggles against her existence as the co-wife of an old man; the widow of

Kuttasammatam ('The Confession') (1940) speaks in defense of her sexual transgression; the female ghost in *Pratikaaradevata* ('The Goddess of Vengeance') (1938) 'explains' the sexual exploits of her past life as a deliberate act of revenge; the young widow of *Jeevitavum Maranavum* ('Life and Death') (1947) turns hysterical rather than be meekly reintegrated into the illam. Hints about such spaces of resistance appear in Nilayamgode's account as well, when she retells how reformist ideas reached the women of her illam—Devaki's sister and her friends could meet the reformist antharjanams who had abandoned traditional dress and ornamentation, and indeed receive information about reformist initiatives precisely because they were travelling alone—without their husbands or brothers. Their training in letters was what helped them to read the pamphlet that the reformist antharjanam had passed them, and their intense seclusion allowed them to hide it from the prying eyes of elders.

The '*Kuriyedathu Tatri*' case of 1905, which exploded the placidity of upper-caste life in Kochi and Malabar, brought the presence of the spaces of subversion for women in traditional life to full public view. The incident mentioned here was the *Smarttavicharam* of the antharjanam named Tatri (Savitri) of the illam called Kuriyedathu, which occurred in 1905. It was exceptional in that she named sixty-four paramours, which included scions of the most esteemed and powerful families of the Malayala Brahmin aristocracy. The extraordinary nature of the case prompted the Raja of Kochi to allow a *Purushavicharam* (a 'trial' in which the accused men were allowed to cross-examine their accuser). But no one escaped. All sixty-four, along with Tatri, were excommunicated. Interestingly, in many autobiographies written by individuals who closely associated with Namboodiri reformism, this incident appears repeatedly as a breaking point—an event that fundamentally changed the way one looked at the world—and Nilayamgode is no exception. More significantly, many believe that modern community-building efforts among the Namboodiris, which culminated in the formation of the Namboodiri Yoga Kshema Sabha in 1908, were an after-effect of the shock produced by the 'Kuriyedathu Tatri' case.

RE-FORMING THE ANTHARJANAM

The *Namboodiri Yoga Kshema Sabha* was formed by Namboodiri aristocrats as an organization for the protection of the interests and privileges enjoyed by Malayala Brahmins threatened by furiously paced social change of the early twentieth century, and for acquisition of necessary skills through modern education. In hindsight, it was hardly 'reformist': the fifth item in its early set of regulations (abandoned later) was that no speech or move should be permitted against existing customs and practices among the Malayala Brahmins. By the 1920s, however, issues of nationalism came to be debated in the YKS annual conferences (such as the conference held at Kulakkada in 1921); the youth wing, the *Namboodiri Yuvajana Sangham*, which was to take radical postures regarding the reorganisation of marriage and family life by the end of the 1920s and early 1930s had become active. By the end of the 1920s, the members of the radical youth wing had begun to argue, among other things, for family reform—for the right of younger men to marry from within caste and set up their own families, for female education and dress reform, for State legislation reforming marriage, inheritance, and partition of joint family holdings—and against prevalent practices like polygamy, marriage of young girls to old men and enforced widowhood (dowry, however, seems to have been criticized only rarely). These positions were articulated in the teeth of opposition from the slower or more orthodox members of the YKS. The pull exerted by nationalism was evident in the career of V.T. Bhattatiripad, who attended the Ahmedabad Conference of the Indian National Congress while yet a student at the special modern school set up at Edakkunni by the YKS for Malayala Brahmin boys. Though strongly influenced by the figure of Gandhi and nationalism, he chose to concentrate on reforming the community. Yet, he was also a vociferous opponent of Malayala Brahmin exclusivity even while retaining a vague sense of Namboodiri-ness and pride in it at times. V.T. and the *Namboodiri Yuvajana Sangham* played an important role in mobilizing public opinion in Malabar in favour of the Congress' Guruvayur Satyagraha. The call to abandon traditional symbols marking caste prestige sparked off tremendous conflict within the YKS in the 1930s.

The transformation of women's lives was high on the radical reformers' agenda, and antharjanams began not only to break traditional codes of conduct but also don the reformer's mantle, becoming a marked presence in reformist meetings. In 1930, Parvati Manezhi, an antharjanam, appeared without *ghosha* at the Edakkunni conference of the YKS, the first antharjanam to do so. Women-reformers like Arya Pallom (who figures in Nilayamgode's account), Parvaty Nenminimangalam, and Devaki Narikkattiri brought in militancy hitherto alien to Malayala Brahmin reformism, and intense efforts to reach antharjanams and introduce them to reformist ideas were made, often under the direct initiative of women-reformers. They were feted as heroines by the liberal public: Parvaty Nenminimangalam was hailed as the 'Joan of Arc of the Namboodiri Empire' by the women's magazine, *The Mahila* in 1932. The formation of the *Antarjana Samajam*, a radical women's wing led by Nenminimangalam, daring propaganda efforts like the Varikkaseri *Varakkattu*—a set of reformist pamphlets circulated at the *Ashtami Rohini Varam* celebrations at Varikkaseri among the antharjanams who were gathered there and elsewhere (these are probably the pamphlets that reached Nilayamgode's sister in 1931)—and 'direct action' to prevent *sambandhams*, marriage of young women to elderly men, and other such practices had far-reaching effects.

By the mid-1930s, however, community reform, it seemed to many, was repudiating community sensibilities—self-correction so dear to reformers, seemed to be replaced by the project of forging a new, radical self altogether. This evoked protest from those who still found merit in adhering to the former. By the late 1930s, many of the most radical voices within the Namboodiri reform movement were moving away from YKS and community reformism itself into leftist politics. Around this time many Malayala Brahmin reformers like E.M.S. Namboodiripad entered leftist politics via the route of community reform and the national movement. For many radical men, the greater acceptance of modern education and the project of modernizing marriage, family, and inheritance within the community signalled the end of the community-reform agenda. Reformism was to be briefly revived in the 1940s after a period of lull largely under leftist initiative, with the reorganization at Ongallur. However, for many women reformers, the project was still not over. Often, their relation with community reformism had been quite different from that of male reformers. Theirs was often a presence which acknowledged that breaking down traditional restrictions constituted just half the journey towards equality and full membership within the community and the larger social world. Thus they often maintained a critical distance from reformism, and their sympathies were clearly marked by this element. For instance, some of the most persuasive constructions of the dreary existence of women in illams and their sheer powerlessness are to be found in the early short stories of Lalitambika Antharjanam; however, some of the most strident critiques of male-oriented reformism, are also to be found in her texts, for example, *Itu Ashasyamano?* ('Is this Desirable?') or *Prasadam* ('Blessed Food'). For these women, the issue of gender equality was not automatically resolved through by merely moving into nationalist or leftist politics. As already quoted, Antharjanam remarked, there were 'many doors' to be broken down before the ideal world of gender equality and gender peace could be attained. In the mid-1940s, some signs that antharjanams had indeed taken up this challenge did appear. *Tozhilkendrathilekku* ('To the Workplace'), a play produced by the Antharjanana Samajam, which declared itself to be the 'first play written by antharjanams for antharjanams', vociferously argued against women's dependence on marriage and their independence through work and wages.

The *Antharjana Samajams* continued to be active—as Nilayamgode's words testify. In the Ongallur meeting E.M.S. Namboodiripad urged Malayala Brahmins to give up traditional aristocratic pride and enter the mainstream of modern Malayalee society as labouring subjects; women too would join by finding means of employment and income. But as Nilayamgode points out, the experiment in employment generation for women was woefully short-lived.

CONCLUSION: HOW OPEN IS THE DOOR?

That her autobiography closes here is something that historians of gender may like to ponder upon, because the vibrant debate in the Malayalee public sphere on gender, its social significance, and the issue of women's attainment of full citizenship began to lose itself in platitudes precisely in the decades in which Nilayamgode chooses to end her story. The limits of 'women's liberation' in elite movements had been reached for Namboodiri women ('antharjanams' no more). The new domestic agency enabled by the modern nuclear family, the (social and familial) 'permission' to be educated and gainful, 'respectable' paid work for family well-being, the access to health care to maintain an efficient labouring and procreative body—all these (clearly ambiguous) gains had been secured by elite women in and through their community movements. As Nilayamgode remarks, there could be '... no autobiography exclusive to antharjanams hereafter'.

Lalitambika Antharjanam would have agreed and disagreed. She would have agreed that upper caste women faced mostly the same challenges. But she continued to remind her readers, well into the 1980s, of the dangers of celebrating too early (as the earlier quote so eloquently puts it). The contrast between her autobiographical musings in *Atmakathaikku Oru Aamugham* ('Preface to an Autobiography') and *Antharjanam* is too striking to be missed. Antharjanam's reminder about the 'many doors' still standing also tells us that the world of upper caste women was not all; that lower caste women faced challenges that are markedly different, and that neither upper-caste reformism nor leftists did justice to lower caste women. Nilayamgode's story, however, tells us, with much precision, exactly how much of the door of tradition was opened to 'free' women of Kerala's modernized elites.

J. Devika

Books Cited

Aiyappan, A., *Social Revolution in a Kerala Village: A Study in Culture Change*. (Bombay: Asia Publishing House, 1965).

Antharjanam, N. Lalitambika, *Atmakathaikku Oru Amugham*. (Thrissur: Current Books, 1991).

_____, *Adyatte Kathakal*. (Kottayam: Sahitya Pravartaka Sahakarana Sangham, 1954, first edition, 1937).

Antharjana Samajam Thrissur, *Tozhilkendrathilekku*. (Thrissur, 1948).

Bhattatiripad, V.T., *Karmavipakam*. (Thrissur: Best Books, 1988).

_____, *Adukkalayil Ninnu Arangathekku*. (Kottayam: D.C. Books, 1994, first edition, 1930).

Kanippayur, N. Sankaran Nambuthiripad, *Ente Smaranakal* vols. I, II, and III. (Kunnamkulam: Panchangom Press, 1965).

KPM, 'Are Women Weak?', in J. Devika (ed. and trans.) *Her-Self: Early Writings on Gender by Malayalee Women*. (Kolkata: Stree, 2005).

Panikkar, T.K. Gopal, *Malabar and its Folk*. (New Delhi: Asian Educational Services, 1983, first edition, 1900).

Report of the Nambuthiri Female Education Commission. (Thrissur: Mangalodayam Press, 1927).

Antharjanam

1 Pakaravoor Illam

I am a seventy-five-year-old *antharjanam* from the Nilayamgode *Illam*. My name is Devaki. I was born in 1928 in Pakaravoor *mana* at Mookkuthala in Malappuram district to Pakaravoor Krishnan Somayajippad and Parvathy Antharjanam. *Achan* was sixty-eight when I was born. I was his twelfth child. During *Amma's* next confinement, Achan passed away at the age of seventy.

I do not remember seeing Achan. But I have heard that though his complexion was dusky, he was handsome and had a certain inner radiance. By the time he married Amma, he was already famous as a *somayaji*, having performed the Vedic ritual of *somayaga* many times. Amma, just eighteen then, was his third wife. But in those days, eighteen was considered late because usually, girls were given in marriage at thirteen or fourteen years of age. Many weddings were arranged even earlier, when they were nine or ten years old. The first time Achan married, he was eighteen. His bride was from Kandanjatha near Vadakkancherry. Her name was Parvathy but she was called Paappi. She had seven or eight children. I can recall five of them: Narayanan, Krishnan, Thuppan, Arya, and Parvathy. Paappi *Valiyamma* died of smallpox. Achan's second wife was Vedic scholar

* Translated by Radhika P. Menon

Erkkara Raman Namboodiri's sister. She died during her first delivery. The baby did not survive either.

That was why Achan was obliged to marry a third time. By then, his eldest son Narayanan was already married and had children. But his wife was unskilled in running the household. So Achan was compelled by his relatives and his aunt to marry again. As Achan's mother was blind, the aunt stayed in the same illam permanently to help manage the house. During those days, there were many blind people in illams.

Achan took his third bride from Karalmanna Naripatta. He did not want any dowry but Naripatta was not prepared to give his daughter away as if she were an orphan. So they found a mutually acceptable solution. It was decided that Achan's three-year-old daughter Parvathy would be given in marriage to Narayanan, the five-year-old son of Naripatta. Thus, an exchange marriage solved the problem of dowry and my fifty-four-year-old Achan gave away his three-year-old daughter, receiving my eighteen-year-old Amma in return. The daughter's wedding, however, took place only after she turned fourteen.

At a time when girls were barely educated, Amma could read the Puranas. The ability to read the Ramayana was itself a major accomplishment. Besides, Amma was an efficient manager of the household. When she came to the illam, my elder (step) sisters had been given away in marriage. But three of Paappi Valiyamma's children were still staying there. And also two *apphan*s—Achan's younger brothers—Parameswaran Namboodiri and Neelakantan Namboodiri. The latter was a great Sanskrit scholar and Vedaratnam Ramerkkara's (Erkkara Raman Namboodiri) guru. During those days, Ramerkkara was staying at the illam to learn Sanskrit. Two *shastri*s or scholar-teachers had been appointed and young Namboodiris who wished to learn Sanskrit stayed in the *pathayappura*. It was like a *gurukulam* with thirty to forty resident scholars—a smaller version of the Sanskrit gurukulam at Koodallur.

Achan too was a Sanskrit scholar. After learning *othu*, the art of reciting the Vedas, he lived as a resident scholar, by turns, in several places and acquired a sound knowledge of Sanskrit. He had spent one or two years at Koodallur as well. Koodallur was a large gurukulam and a seat of profound learning. It had an enormous collection of books. Many shastris from Tamil Nadu had been appointed there and they used to pay regular visits. A large number of students stayed at Koodallur. Their expenses—food, clothes, and recreation—were met from the pooled assets of the Brahmin community called the *Brahmaswam*. Achan, 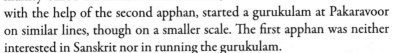 with the help of the second apphan, started a gurukulam at Pakaravoor on similar lines, though on a smaller scale. The first apphan was neither interested in Sanskrit nor in running the gurukulam.

The young Namboodiri students who stayed at our illam stepped indoors only during meal times. As Pakaravoor was a prosperous household, two Namboodiris were engaged to prepare food and a Tamil Brahmin was employed solely to make snacks. In those days, Namboodiris did not eat rice cooked by Tamil Brahmins. There was also an antharjanam, sometimes two or more, who stayed at the illam to help in assembling puja items for daily worship. Besides, there were *irikkanamma*s, main companions of antharjanams, who took turns to be at the illam to supervise the household chores. When one of them came to stay, she brought her whole family along.

Although its *naalukettu* was rather small, our illam was very spacious. However, only its western section had an upper storey. Achan constructed three new buildings, a *nataka shala* for staging performances like the Kathakali and four large porticos. Each building had a big kitchen attached to it which we called the *oottuppura*. There was a large oottuppura where coffee was brewed. One could sit there, lean against the railing, and enjoy coffee. The nataka shala could serve meals to a thousand people at a time.

One of the porticos was exclusively for Namboodiris and they sat there to chew betel leaves. All the ingredients were lined up on the ledge and spittoons were placed around the portico. It was there that the Namboodiris assembled and swapped stories.

So the building always echoed with loud conversations and laughter. Another portico was for the estate managers. A room adjoining it served as their office. It took five to six managers to keep the accounts of the illam and collect rents from properties. Whenever they felt tired, they went to the portico to relax. The largest portico served as a place to rest for Namboodiris, both before and after meals. It stood closest to the kitchen. The pathayappura, which was a regular haunt of Namboodiris—inmates of the illam as well as outsiders—opened straight into this portico. The number of people who arrived for meals always varied. There were many of them—the residents themselves, devotees who came to pray at the temple, passers-by, and so on.

The fourth portico was located behind the western block, close to the storehouse. It was long and shaped almost like a corridor with a ledge running along its entire length. The store managers and servants occupied it. It was here that the store manager sat with sacks of rice, to dole out a certain measure of grain to needy persons who approached him. Many women and children streamed in and the manager remained in the portico till the flow of people ceased.

Among the retainers at the illam, the person next in importance to the manager was a man we called the 'monkey scarer'. In the grove near Mookkuthala temple, there lived a large colony of monkeys. They came regularly in huge numbers to sit on the rooftop of the illam. It was fun to watch them as they removed lice from each other's fur, fondled their babies, and emitted strange shrieks. Seeing the red faces of the she-monkeys, we used to think that they had applied a paste of brick powder on their faces as a cosmetic. But we were alarmed whenever the monkeys entered the illam. As we sat to have lunch, they squeezed themselves in through the gap between the wall and the attic, fell on us, and scampered away dragging our plantain leaves laden with food. Often we ran out, screaming. The adult monkeys, with the young ones clinging to their backs and bellies, used the babies' paws to scoop the hot *payasam*, spread the sweet pudding out to cool, took mouthfuls of it, and then left. This was a regular sight. In order to prevent their entry into the illam, the 'monkey scarer' constantly patrolled the courtyard. Armed with many stones and a catapult, he marched up and down and shouted to drive them away. As the lunch hour approached, he became more alert and paced about faster.

Besides the residents, those who came regularly to have meals at the illam were antharjanams on their way to Mookkuthala temple or back. Each had a chaperone who led the way, shouting '*Yaa ... hey ... yaa ... hey ...*'. These sounds were meant to alert unwary passers-by belonging to lower castes, who could then move out of the way so as not to cause the antharjanams any pollution.

The visitors stayed on for three or four days. No one asked them to leave. There was a large hall meant for their use and it had a single huge rush-mat that covered the entire floor. By dusk, an irikkanamma spread it out. It reeked with the stench of children's urine and soiled clothes. Sometimes, my elder sisters also lay down on that mat. Nothing was specially set apart for the illam inmates. In the mornings, the irikkanammas swept the mat with a broom to remove the dust, folded it over and over and put it aside. It was in this hall that several groups of older girls played games with pebbles at different times of the day. In the evenings, young girls danced the *Kaikottikkali*.

The visiting antharjanams were considered polluted on arrival and had to first take a purifying bath. Dressed in wet clothes, they went to the temple and then returned to the illam. Every year, eight to ten lengths of new cloth were bought at Pakaravoor for such guests. The antharjanams then left their wet clothes on the line in the veranda. Those bits of clothing hung like festoons swaying in the breeze.

It was into this huge illam that Amma was led but she was adept at managing it. She was a very serious woman. Her children never once saw her laugh.

Achan was bedridden for about six months before he died. His room was near a portico, at some distance from the veranda used by the antharjanams. Going against the practice generally followed in illams those days, Achan insisted that Amma attend on him. She obeyed, leaving her baby in the care of another antharjanam who stayed in the illam. My younger sister grew up suckled by that lady.

Achan was very particular about providing food for as many people as possible. However, that practice waned after his death. Huge vessels lay unused in the oottuppuras, gathering dust and cobwebs. Gradually, the number of visitors dwindled and with that, the large rush mat also vanished.

I was the sixth of Amma's seven children. My three brothers and two sisters are: Neelakantan, Chithran, Parameswaran, Nangeli, and Unnikkali. The seventh died in childhood. Named Unneema, she was the most beautiful among us and the most energetic. She lived for ten years at the illam and was the darling of the family. Then one day, she suddenly fell ill and lay in bed for three days. Unneema died without receiving any medical attention. I remember how I paid my respects to the little corpse, bathed and dressed in new clothes before cremation.

In those days, the birth of a girl in illams was not considered auspicious. As soon as a woman became pregnant, there were special prayers and pujas for a baby boy. If the child was a boy, servants ululated and announced the happy event. If a girl, irikkanammas conveyed the news with soft knocks on the door and in muted whispers.

I was born on *Thiruvonam* day in the month of *Idavam*. There were no joyous shouts that day, only soft knocks on doors.

2 *Amma*

Amma, as I remember her, always looked very grave. We, her children, could never read her mind. So we contented ourselves by loving and respecting her from a distance without ever trying to get close.

As the efficient wife of the celebrated and powerful Pakaravoor Krishnan Somayajippad, she was respected both within the family and amongst the townspeople. Even *Achan's* first wife's children and other members of the *illam* could not find fault with Amma's housekeeping. Despite her husband being much older, her seventeen years with him gave her status much dignity.

The situation changed after Achan died. Those who had treated her with respect till then began to slight her. A widow with her eldest son aged only fifteen and six younger children to care for, she was helpless and insecure. But she displayed extraordinary will power and held herself together.

Boys were considered family assets and their wants were taken care of by the household. So Amma's three sons were brought up with all the comforts that the other children enjoyed. But when they grew up and began to actively participate in progressive social movements, the conservative elders of our family rejected them and blamed her for not

* Translated by Indira Menon

having disciplined them in their formative years. However, she would not disown them.

Amma was worried about us, her girls. She did not have the money to satisfy even our slightest demands. When we consider the situation that the *antharjanams* found themselves in, this was not surprising. A man who married late in life, fathered several children, and died suddenly, did not have to worry about how his family fared afterwards. It was believed that they would survive if the household had enough food to eat. This must have been the case with my Achan too.

It was when we fell ill that Amma was most concerned. She would then send Narayani, the maidservant, to consult the village apothecary and fetch the prescribed medicines. Minor ailments were cured in this way.

One day, my younger sister was taken ill. She was feverish and had a stomach upset. The apothecary's medicines did not help and she was weakening rapidly. For the first time, Amma forced her eldest son to inform the men of the family about her daughter's condition. *Ettan* reluctantly approached the Namboodiris who had assembled in the hall for their banter with her request for medical assistance. In reply, they laughed at him and passed caustic remarks; he returned, unsuccessful, to her.

The next night, our sister lay weak and helpless in the *vadakkini* as we went to sleep in our *vadakke ara*. In the early hours of the morning, Amma woke me up and said in a low tone: 'The child is very ill. Come and prostrate before her.' I wondered how this would help to cure her. When I went there, she had already been placed on the floor, her head pointed in the direction towards the south. Though perplexed and still uncomprehending, it was clear to me that something untoward had happened. Trembling inwardly, I prostrated before her. This was my first encounter with death. I knew only later that though the dead child was younger, we were required to show our respect because she had preceded us in death.

Amma was adamant that the child be given the same funeral rites as a grown person. There were some things to be observed while welcoming death. Several oil lamps were lit in the house. Two rows of lighted wicks were placed all the way to the southern entrance. Brahmins were given offerings to facilitate the journey of the soul. Amma muttered to herself, 'If she must go, let it be with grace.'

When it was over, she came to my room, lay down by my side, and, for the first time in my life, held me close to her. I had never slept beside her before. She was trying to control her sobs because I could feel her stomach press and heave against mine.

It was on the fortieth day after this sister's birth that my Achan was taken ill and was confined to the room adjoining the entrance. Amma entrusted the newborn to the antharjanam cook, shed the clothes worn in the labour room, and, taking a bath, set out to nurse him. Achan lay ill in bed for six months and all the time, till he died, she took care of him. His death depressed her.

Perhaps because Amma felt guilty for having neglected her child, depriving her of mother's milk and tenderness, she started paying some attention to me after that, as if apologizing for withholding love.

A tragic event occurred in our neighbouring illam—the Mangalatheri family who were related to us. Our mothers had come to Mookkuthala at the same time. They had also grown close because they met regularly at the temple and other places. One day, her two grown sons died of typhoid within hours of each other. Treatment in those days did not always take the seriousness of the illness into account. Usually, typhoid caused high fever and the patient would be unconscious for several days. But these young men lasted only one week. Death came suddenly, unexpectedly. They had been active in the Mookkuthala library and had participated in progressive social movements, being of the same age as Amma's children.

Pakaravoor heard this shocking news one afternoon. Immediately, Amma picked up the *mundu* hanging on the clothesline in the vadakkini, covered herself with it, and, carrying an umbrella, hurried to the house of death. On seeing her agitated state, an *irikkanamma* set out to follow her. She had to cover two miles to reach their house where she spent the day without food, searching for words to comfort them. Amma continued to be distressed for a long time. Though it was of no real use, she visited them regularly for several days afterwards.

Amma helped the poor by giving them clothes from her trunk and all the food they could eat. She had no money to assist them financially but she would console them with her words. They would say that they took heart from her reassuring presence.

She did not give us, her daughters, any freedom because she believed that girls should not be encouraged to think and act independently. This was the time after the *smaarthavichaaram* or trial by religious rituals of Kuriyedathu Thaatri by Brahmin priests. Suspected of adultery she had implicated some of Amma's relatives resulting in grave injustice to their families. Nangemma Nangyar was among those affected and even at birth was excommunicated for her father's crime. Amma treated her with special consideration and a lot of affection, sometimes saying to herself that the girl had no one of her own. As she lay dying, Amma directed us to make provision at the Guruvayoor temple for Nangemma to be given meals everyday throughout her life.

She did not, for all her orthodoxy, support the discrimination against girls. In an illam nearby, an antharjanam had given birth to twin girls leading to consternation in that family as if a great calamity had befallen them. Amma went there to console her. 'Don't worry. Bring up your children well. The rest will be as fate decrees.'

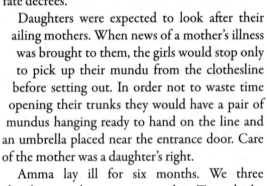

Daughters were expected to look after their ailing mothers. When news of a mother's illness was brought to them, the girls would stop only to pick up their mundu from the clothesline before setting out. In order not to waste time opening their trunks they would have a pair of mundus hanging ready to hand on the line and an umbrella placed near the entrance door. Care of the mother was a daughter's right.

Amma lay ill for six months. We three daughters took turns to nurse her. Towards the end, the antharjanam from Koodalloor whom Amma respected, came to see her. She sat down near her and asked about her condition. Quite unexpectedly, Amma said, 'Tell me what one who is dying must do.' Koodallooramma was taken aback. She spoke softly: 'Rid your mind of unwanted thoughts to purify it. Pray if you can.'

Amma may have accepted that advice on her last journey.

3 The Daily Routine

Like all the children of Pakaravoor Illam, I was raised by irikkanammas. We were seven children born to Amma and six to Valiyamma. A few Nair women, six or seven, lived in the illam to look after us. They took care of us till the pre-puberty ritual of *uduthu thudangal* was performed, usually at the age of nine.

Following the prevailing custom, there were separate groups of women to look after the children of each antharjanam. One member of each group was considered its leader and the rest took orders from her. Amma's children were looked after by Aati and her daughters—Ittippennu and Ichirippennu, with Aati as the leader.

Amma suckled me only for a year and I was soon transferred to Aati's care. The servants did everything for the babies, except feeding and suckling them. Being Shudra women, they were not supposed to breastfeed us. Sometimes, antharjanams from other places were brought to Pakaravoor to serve as wet-nurses. This arrangement was made if the mother became pregnant within a year of childbirth and the one-year-old baby was a boy. When the wet-nurses came to stay, they brought their children with them. These antharjanams usually went to prosperous illams when life in their

* Translated by Radhika P. Menon

own became intolerable due to poverty, neglect, or harassment from co-wives. But as wet-nurses, they were given preferential treatment.

One often heard commands like 'Serve those wet-nurses more food ... let them have an oil bath ...' Sumptuous meals and elaborate oil baths were considered good for plentiful breast milk. Thus, suckling their own children only for a short while, these wet-nurses reserved the rest for the infants of the illam.

However, when breast milk was not available, children were not given cow's milk. This was not because of any shortage at the illam; in fact, there was plenty of it. I remember the store-manager Nambisan sitting with a cauldron, or the *nilaathu*, by his side in the portico next to the storehouse. One of his duties was to collect cow's milk from the neighbourhood. Achan's standing order was to accept all the milk brought to the illam. Before noon, the nilaathu would brim over. It took two men to transfer the vessel to the kitchen. Besides this, there was the milk that servants drew from the cows the illam owned. A large measure of it went to the Tamil Brahmin's kitchen for preparing coffee.

The milk thus collected was never meant for children. Weaned within a year of their birth, most of them looked pale and consumptive. Still, cow's milk was strictly taboo. It was used to make ghee in which lamps were lit at the temple and to make buttermilk for preparing *kaalan*, a curry served at feasts in the illam. All the buttermilk and butter were made by irikkanammas in the kitchen. A small quantity of the ghee, made from butter, was stored away to serve the Namboodiris at lunch and the rest was sent to the temple.

Buttermilk was diluted and served as *sambhaaram* during lunch. Sometimes, at night when little children cried of hunger, they were given two gulps of sambhaaram. That was the nature of childcare in those days. Everyone believed that the light from the ghee-lamps glowing in the temple was enough to ensure the children's health and prosperity.

One of the main daily chores of Aati, Ittippennu, and Ichirippennu was making loincloths of plantain leaves for small children. When the children grew older, they were given loincloths of *koombala*, the tender film of the arecanut spathe. Up to the age of eight, we girls wore the leaf-loincloth. Two pieces of a plantain leaf, warmed over a fire to make them soft and pliable, were tied together to fashion a loincloth. As the sun grew hotter

it gradually lost its softness, became fibrous, and chaffed the skin badly. But the koombala loincloth was softer and lasted longer. We could never use cloth for this purpose because it was believed that a Nair woman's touch polluted any garment made of cloth. Any such material would have to be discarded. Therefore, until the time of uduthu thudangal for girls and *upanayanam* for boys, the children at the illam never wore loincloths made of cotton.

It was the responsibility of Aati and others to prepare plantain and koombala loincloths every night. Morning baths over, we were made to wear them and taken to the temples. They carried us on their hips to the Melekkavu, Keezhekkavu, Kannankkavu, and Pakaravoor Shiva temples. However, we enjoyed this privilege only up to the age of four. After that, we had to walk the entire distance. Once a month, boys had to go to the village temple at Shukapuram as well. Servants usually carried young boys on their shoulders, holding their legs firmly while the boys wrapped their arms round the men's foreheads.

By the time we returned from the temple, the sun would be high in the sky. The maids then took the children indoors for breakfast which was, unvaryingly, steaming rice with buttermilk and mango pickles. By the time we finished our breakfast, Aati and others would have had theirs, usually the previous day's gruel. The four and five-year-old were then permitted to play in the courtyard or the garden. And there they remained till noon, engrossed in games, with maidservants watching over them.

Girls were served lunch only after the Namboodiris, children, young mothers, and menstruating women were given their meals.

Cooked rice, dishes like sautéed vegetables, kaalan, and mango pickles comprised our lunch. For the antharjanams, this was their day's first meal. After the customary temple visit, they had to prepare offerings for the deity and therefore had little spare time. The servants would have had at least the previous day's gruel for breakfast. But not the mothers and other antharjanams. After the children's turn, it was time to serve outsiders—servants, the Nair retainers, and so on. Everyone was served a lot more than they could eat. The maids ate only a small portion of what they received and sent the rest to their homes. There was a special room in the illam called *chottara* to store their containers. By afternoon, the chottara would be full of brass vessels of cooked rice. Late afternoons and early evenings, the older girls were trained to make garlands of *karuka* grass and prepare lamp-wicks. By dusk, everyone had to wash their faces and feet in the pond and assemble in the naalukettu where a heap of ten varieties of flowers or the *dashapushpam* was kept ready. The girls had to identify each type and tie them into separate garlands. The karuka garland had a special significance in an antharjanam's life. She had to wear it on all special occasions like her birthday, wedding day, and so on. Not one of the ten flowers had either colour or fragrance. Colourful and sweet-smelling flowers were used only in the pujas for the deities in the northern wing of the naalukettu or in the temple. Antharjanams never wore flowers.

Though clocks were rare in those days, there was one at our illam, but it was placed in the pathayappura. So the illam inmates had to go out into the courtyard to measure the length of the shadow or look at a star in order to calculate

the time. When they counted five
feet on the shadow, it was time
to prepare the karuka garlands.
In the meanwhile, coffee and
snacks were served—only
to resident Namboodiris,
guests and students—in the
oottuppura. The Tamil Brahmin
prepared coffee and several snacks
like *aval kuzhachathu, kaarolappom, ada,
malarpodi*, and so on. A small portion of
these reached the inner rooms and were distributed among us.

Once, when I was five or six years old, some of us found the wafting
aroma of roasted coffee beans so overpowering that we longed to drink
coffee. So one day, we secretly entered the kitchen and stole some coffee
powder and sugar. We also managed to take away a huge quantity of
thick milk that the store manager Nambisan had left on the stove. Under
my elder sister's supervision, we started making coffee behind closed
doors. But just as we finished preparing it, we heard a knock at the door.
Whenever Namboodiris entered the naalukettu, they usually announced
their presence by clanging the chain that hung from the door. It was a
warning to some antharjanams to keep out of sight. From the pattern of
sound, we knew it was *Valiyettan*, our elder brother. We fled to the side
room which served as a urinal, taking the coffee and all the vessels with
us. After he walked away, we stood behind the closed door and, still
trembling, drank the coffee. But by then, it had gone cold.

In the evenings, after bath, we went to Melekkavu to pray. On returning home, we smeared sacred ash on our foreheads and chanted the
Namashivaya, praising Lord Shiva. When the glass tile on the kitchen
roof turned dark, it was time for dinner. *Pulinkari*, sautéed vegetables,
pickles, and buttermilk were served with rice. Thereafter, the maids un-
rolled the mats along the corridor floors. It was time for children to go to
sleep. That brought the day's activities to a close. And the same routine
was repeated day after day.

4 The Ritual Bath

Amma was my father's third wife. His first wife's son Narayanan—
Valiyettan to us—was older than Amma. Valiyettan's son Unni was exactly
the same age as my own elder brother. His mother Parvathi, though a
sister by marriage, was called Unnidamma, Unni's mother, by all of us.

Valiyettan had been ill for five or six months before he died. I'm not
sure what his illness was. Those days, I don't think people understood or
cared about the real nature of any illness. It must have been something
serious because Dr Krishna Iyer was called in when Ayurvedic medicines
failed. Valiyettan was sixty at the time and his wife was fifty-two.

I can still picture the widowed Unnidamma returning from a bath in
the pond, soaking wet, dripping water as she walked to the *vadakke ara*.
This room was badly lit even in the best of times. Now even the narrow
windows with their thick bars which let in some light were shut. Widows
had to sit in a dark room such as this, during *pula*, the period of defilement, shut away from others. Most people were reluctant to see them in
their newly widowed state, their necks bare of a '*thaali*'. So only the closest
relatives went up to the door to meet them.

After a bath, widows would not change out of their wet clothes which
they also used as sheets to sleep on. Eventually, the warmth of the body may

* Translated by Indira Menon

have dried these a little. The bath was not just once, but three times a day. The first one was at dawn and after this, they would not rub themselves dry but merely squeeze some water out of their clothes. In the meantime, the son would have performed the rites following a death in the *nadumittam*, the central courtyard of the house, after which the widow would take a second bath. Again she would not dry herself. The evening bath was the last prescribed one.

After the period of the pula, Unni's mother observed *deeksha* with her son for a year, when she was required to have two baths every day.

The bath was the most significant of the Namboodiri practices. It was considered the corrective for all defilement—whether it was hearing the news of the pula or the preceding death, or merely a visit to the house of death. Even without this, it often became obligatory to have a bath several times a day. Therefore, *illam*s had two tanks—one on the *vadakkupuram*, north-eastern side near the kitchen for the antharjanams and another on the *thekkupuram*, southern side for the Namboodiris. If there was a temple attached to the illam, there would be a temple-tank as well, common to all.

The antharjanams would set out for the kitchen-tank before sunrise. If the light was insufficient, the *irikkanamma* would walk ahead of them carrying a long-handled oil lamp. They would brush their teeth in the tank with *umikkeri* and the leaves of the mango tree served as a tongue-scraper. After this, the married women would chew betel leaves with lime and arecanut, but without tobacco which they did not usually add to the three ingredients. Then they would spit it out into the tank and get into the water for their bath. Oil was applied only on Tuesdays and Fridays unless the birth-stars of their husbands or sons fell on that day. After the oil massage, the irikkanamma would crush some medicinal leaves to make a herbal shampoo. She would also scrub the antharjanams' back with the rough-textured *vaaka* which invigorated them. After taking several dips, they would emerge from the water and, seated on the steps leading to the tank, apply a paste of castor seeds and turmeric on their forehead. A final dip was prescribed before they rubbed themselves dry with a towel.

Some of them opted to pray standing waist-deep in the water, their hair firmly tied back. It was easier bowing their heads down to the level of their feet in water rather than on a hard floor. This would last an hour. When the Namboodiris prayed they chanted mantras from the Vedas and other religious books. But since women were excluded from such learning, they were able to recite only a few *shlokas* as prayer.

During this time, if someone who had not had a bath, or a lower-caste Shudra who was washing clothes, happened to splash some water on them, the antharjanams were required to go for another dip in the tank. If they trod on some strands of hair on the stone steps, yet another bath became unavoidable. They would, therefore, encourage the irikkanamma's daughters to keep the area clean and the incentive offered was their assurance that the girls would be reborn as beautiful maidens if they did their bidding. Again, if they stepped on a thread or hair or spittle, or if they suspected that untouchables had brushed past them on their way to the temple or back home, only a bath could restore their purity.

Within the illam, too, the bath became unavoidable in special circumstances. If they picked up the vessels washed and stacked in the kitchen the previous night by the irikkanamma and found them inadequately cleaned, another bath became imperative. The other grounds were: stepping on the floor if it had not been purified with cow dung after a meal, accidentally brushing against the servants while at work, or the servant's clothes fluttering over the antharjanam. The list was long. Menstruating women had to have a ritual bath on the fourth day.

But the most distressing of all was the traditional bath after delivering a child. The woman would usually be desperately thirsty soon after giving birth, even before the placenta was expelled, but would not be allowed any water because the midwife who attended on her belonged to the lower-class barber community and had sullied her by her touch. So the first thing the antharjanam was forced to do would be to walk to the kitchen tank even if it was far away and take a bath. Others would help her to get there but, on the way back, she would have to negotiate the steps alone and return to her room without touching them. In summer months, the water level would have dropped and the tank filled with slush and mud. But this was no deterrent. It did not occur to anyone that perhaps a bath in muddy water could lead to infection. The woman would come back weak and pale, thirsting for some water.

On the eleventh day after the birth, the purification ceremony was conducted, after which the woman was considered cleansed, signalling the start of the therapeutic baths. These continued for ninety days and were thoroughly enjoyable. Twice a day the new mother would have a bath in water in which the leaves of various trees like *pullani*, jackfruit, mango, castor, and the *ungu* were boiled together. A water outlet was made on the northern side of the illam and a wooden plank placed at one end for the woman to sit on. The antharjanam who was employed to give a bath would smear oil on the new mother and give her a massage. Then she would cup the hot water (leaves included) in her palm, scrub the mother with it, work up a lather with powdered *inja* to remove excess oil, and rinse it off with some of the hot water. Inja is the bark of a tree which is beaten to the consistency of fibre and foams when moistened. Its rough texture is believed to increase blood circulation. Next, she would pour the hot water along with the leaves on the antharjanam, smear a paste of fresh turmeric all over her, and wash her with the remaining hot water. For a month, this final rinse would be done with water in which *nalpamara* was boiled, designed to increase her beauty. Her hair was not washed every day, but gingelly oil was applied regularly to cool the head. This was also considered effective in increasing breast milk.

The ninety-day period of such luxurious baths was the best time in an antharjanam's life. They were free of the daily drudgery, baths were given twice a day for improved health, and special attention was accorded by a person appointed for this. It was as if she had suddenly become a person of consequence.

There were also ritual baths following a death. The body was lowered to the floor and cleansing water poured over it. Then three people would be required to touch the dead one and go for a customary dip in the tank. This would be repeated three times. After that, the body—referred to usually as the *pretham*—was thought to be purified and ready for cremation.

I arrived in Nilayamgode after my wedding in 1943. My father-in-law, Ravi Somayajippad, had died two years earlier. He had been famous in his youth as a Kathakali dancer till he married and restricted his activities to performing *yagam*. Paapti *Valiamma* never tired of narrating the astonishing story of how he was given a bath before he died.

When he died, my father-in-law must have been nearly sixty years old. Being a Somayajippad, he used to conduct the *Agnihotra homam* daily in the illam's *vadakkini*. His last wish was that, when was dying, he should be placed near these homam fires, which meant that all traditional rites were to be observed after his death. All Somayajis were placed on the floor near the homam fires when they were dying.

But there was a peculiar problem with the vadakkini. It was a sanctified place of worship and nobody was allowed inside without a bath. How could *Achan*, who was lying in an outer room, be moved to the vadakkini? How could he be taken to the tank to be given a bath? A person could be shifted to the vadakkini only when death was certain and the last few breaths were being exhaled. If he was taken at that juncture for a dip in the tank, the family might well be accused of drowning him. Nobody knew what to do. By then, Achan, lying in the outer room, had begun to draw his last breaths. In the vadakkini, antharjanams spread *darbha* grass and sand near the homam pits and started a fire in all three of them. They lit oil lamps and prepared to lower him to the floor. Namboodiris prepared to recite mantras in his ear. There was no time to discuss options. If he wanted to die in the vadakkini, he must be given a bath. He was lifted onto a long wooden plank and taken down to the last step leading to the tank. His third son, Ravi Namboodiri, who later became my husband, picked up his Achan as he would a child and walked into the water to give him a dip. All the Namboodiris who had carried him entered the water simultaneously for a bath. Fortunately, Achan was still alive. Then, they brought him to the vadakkini on the same wooden plank, placed him on the darbha grass, started chanting mantras in his ear, and made offerings for his final journey. Achan died peacefully. This being an extraordinarily eventful bath, the Nilayamgode family members recounted the story to me several times over.

5 Clothes

In my birthplace Pakaravoor, a *plashu* tree stood in the south-western corner of the wide brick-tiled space between the *nalukettu* and the *pathayappura*. A large tree with widespread branches and plentiful shady leaves, it was protected by a built-up base about three feet high. This provided us with a playing area.

Plashu is a sacred tree found near temples and Brahmin houses. Its branches are used to stoke the *homam* fires. They are essential to the evening rituals performed by young Namboodiris, and in the period leading to their *upanayanam* these boys are required to have the stems ready to hand. Therefore bundles of its twigs and darbha grass for use in vedic rituals were stored in a square frame tied together with a rope and hung up in the *vadakkini*. Servants climbed on the tall tree to break off the twigs, dried them in the sun, and stored them inside. Thus, the plashu tree was considered indispensable and great care was taken to safeguard it.

The tree flowered at regular intervals. A veil of yellow-tinged orange flowers concealing the leaves bloomed during the day and cascaded down in the evening and night, shrouding the brick-lined earth. In my childhood, this sight fascinated me. Early in the morning before the place was swept clean, we'd gather these flowers in a leaf bowl just for the fun of it,

* Translated by Indira Menon

to admire the colours. The petals were long and very fragile. They had to be picked up with great care because they stuck to the brick-floor where they fell. But while we were merely fascinated by the blooms there were those who had use for them. Our mothers wanted them for their puja which lasted all morning. Various kinds of flowers like *thechi*, *mandaram*, *thamara*, *nandyarvattam*, *shankupushpam* both blue and white, *alari*, *chembaruthi*, *koovalam* leaves, three types of *thulasi*, and also the plashu flower were required for this puja. Plashu flowers were in great demand with our washerwomen as well.

The services of these women who belonged to the Veluthedath family were as invaluable to the antharjanam as their irikkanammas. They were generally addressed in short as '*veluthedath ullaval*'. But the women of Pakaravoor called them affectionately by their names: Lakshmi, Cheetha, Chinna. There was a reason why their services were so highly valued. On an everyday basis, the antharjanams would pound their clothes on the steps of the tank, rinse them in the water and hang them out to dry on the clothesline tied to the *utharam* surrounding the *nadumittam*. They did not use soap. The walk to the temple over muddy paths and the dung-smeared *illam* floors on which they sat, made the clothes look shabby and grey. The antharjanams who dressed very simply without any redeeming colour, must have longed to ensure that their clothes remained white. Therefore the washerwomen were eagerly welcomed when they arrived in the illam. Not only did the antharjanams give them their washing, but also evinced keen interest in their family matters—their older children's weddings, the younger ones' illnesses, the welfare of their elderly relatives.

The mother was called Lakshmi, and Cheetha and Chinna were her daughters. As far back as I can remember, Cheetha was either pregnant or carried an infant baby on her hip. She had ten children. Whenever there was a festive occasion in the illam, they were given their share of the food to take home. At such times, Amma would force Cheetha to eat more, saying that what she consumed was not just for her alone. Amma meant either the breastfed baby or the one in the womb.

Lakshmi and her daughters would appear in our backyard dressed neatly with their hair tied up at an angle and their lips red with chewing betel leaves. Though they were constantly exposed to the elements, moving as they did between water ponds and grassy slopes, their appearance seemed untouched by the sun and the wind beating down on them. They were always pleased with the solicitous enquiries of the antharjanams when they arrived carrying bundles of washed *mundus* neatly folded and marked individually with the ink from the nut tree. These were considered to be purified if the veluthedath ullaval handled them. The clothes worn during travel were declared unpolluted even without their being dipped in water if a pinch of the ash they brought was sprinkled over them.

The women came with the cleaned clothes once a week. As they were not allowed to wash clothes in the illam tank or in the one adjoining the temple, they had to walk long distances to a water body in the fields to do the washing. The clothes were first boiled in water to which caustic soda and ash were added and beaten on rough stone to remove the dirt and restore their sheen. After the wash, they were dipped in water mixed with the blue powder which they carried wrapped in a small cloth bag, and later spread out to dry on the grass or on the rocks to reclaim their pristine whiteness. The process of starching them came later. For this purpose, the women were given a measure of paddy which had to be hand-pounded and boiled for a long time till the liquid thickened to starch in which the mundus, the *pudava* and the longer cloth used as a cloak were all immersed and then stretched out to dry. The *pavumundu*, called 'thirudayada' worn by the deity during temple festivals, needed special treatment since the garment had to be folded in several layers till it could be opened out in the shape of a fan and placed around the idol during the procession. The cooked, hand-pounded rice from which the starch was drawn was strained through a clean towel tied around the mouth of a vessel. It was then squeezed out through the cloth by hand, the remaining rice made into balls, and put aside for their dogs. Its nutritious quality must have been the reason why the veluthedath dogs looked healthy and well-groomed. These dogs guarded the clothes spread out to dry in the fields and on the rocks. They were big and looked threatening but were not aggressive. However, I was afraid of the one called 'Tippu' which followed Cheetha around. The dogs went with them everywhere.

Unlike most other Namboodiris, Achan insisted on wearing fresh white clothes every day. Therefore a Veluthedath family was given a place to stay in the eastern part of the grounds, the *kizhakkupuram,* and, to this day, that piece of land is called the Veluthedath compound. There was a building adjoining the tank with a small window on the ground floor attached to a box fixed to the wall. This window could be opened both ways, from inside and outside. Every morning, Lakshmi's son would open the window from outside and place freshly washed, starched, and neatly folded mundu, towel, and loincloth in the box. After his bath, Achan would go up the steps wearing his wet clothes, open the window from inside, and change into the clean clothes to be ready for the temple. He used to wear *'illikunnan'* mundu which was considered to be the best quality at the time. It stayed fresh throughout the day and was said to have lent added dignity to his personality.

Our mothers were very pleased with the starched, white clothes arranged neatly in the wooden slat-enclosed veranda at the back of the house. The marking on the clothes ensured that these were stacked in individual piles. For this work, the Veluthedath family was given a regular salary as also several rights and perquisites. In addition, the antharjanams, eager to please them, plied them with extra food on special occasions. During a feast, they would put aside *pappadams,* ripe bananas, and fried banana chips, as well as fried yam for these dear ones. On such occasions, Lakshmi and Cheetha would carry baskets overflowing with these offerings. Since they did not have any money of their own, the antharjanams expressed their affection and gratitude in this manner. When there was a festival like the Pooram Ganapati celebration, each one competed with the other in giving them sweets like *appam* and *ada.*

There was another reason for this generosity. The antharjanams had two or three special pudavas to be worn at weddings and on important occasions. This pudava was gifted to them as new brides and they wore it when they entered their future homes after four days of wedding rituals. A *chittu* for their earlobes and a small *thaali* to be worn round the neck were also given by the bridegrooms' family. The grandeur of the pudava would be in keeping with their family status. It was woven out of the finest threads, a garment as long and wide as two mundus joined together. A gold-coloured border of the width of a finger and a narrow black one on the upper and lower edges added to its beauty. Broad stripes evenly spaced across the width of the garment adorned the pudava at five different points. The designs comprised *ezhuthanikkara*, *veppilachutti*, and such others. My second older sister Unikkali's bridegroom had brought her an extra special pudava which she has carefully preserved to this day. The gold-coloured border was three fingers wide and, in addition it, had parrots and lotus flowers woven with gold thread. The fine cloth, the ezhuthanikkara and veppilachutti enhanced by a broad gold border between, and the parrot and lotus motifs were indicative of the quality of the pudava and signalled the status of the family. They were woven in Tamil Nadu and Veeramani Swami of Pattambi was credited with bringing them to Kerala.

Such pudavas needed extra care while being washed. Antharjanams would take them out of their boxes the moment an invitation to attend a wedding was extended. Every antharjanam owned a heavy box made of the wood of the jackfruit tree and decorated with brass fittings. This was her only personal possession. At the bottom of the box, she would scatter a measure of black peppercorns, some shavings of sandalwood, and the medicinal root *vayambu*, over which was spread a fine towel to preserve the pudavas on top. Even after seventy years, the peppercorns in my sister's box have retained their pungency. They are the preservers of the pudavas put away till further use. Sometimes, *kaithapoo* was also placed inside for fragrance. The folded and stored pudavas were given to the veluthedath ullaval for starching and burnishing the gold border. The pudava was dipped in carefully made starch, spread out to dry and the wrinkles gently teased out with a long heavy stick. Then came the process of *poovidal* to give sheen to the gold border. This border had shining white interwoven threads which appeared unattractive till expert washerwomen lent colour and lustre to it, causing an amazing transformation.

This magic was created by the plashu flower. The flower was crushed in the palm and a pinch of turmeric and lime paste added to form a mixture which was smeared on the silver border to make it shine like gold. The kind of gold-bordered mundu called *kottaram kasavu* seen today was forbidden to the antharjanams. My *apphan*'s daughters, Bharathi and Subhadra from the Ekkanath family, wore these kottaram kasavu mundus when they visited the illam. But the antharjanams had to be satisfied with the gold colour of the plashu flower.

The plashu tree did not flower throughout the year. Therefore the flowers were picked, dried, and stored carefully in small boxes. Amma would often insist that we give the flowers we gathered to Lakshmi.

Rubbing the plashu juice on the border precisely and gently was an art at which Cheetha was adept. Our mothers were often insistent that she did the poovidal for them. Care had to be exercised that the yellowish orange colour was spread evenly on the lines, that it did not smudge the rest of the material, and that it seeped in to cause the silver threads to sparkle like gold. The pudavas of fine material with their ezhuthanikkara and vepillachutti woven in black and the specially designed parrots and lotuses starched and ironed out with a heavy rod, would be exhibited majestically on the wooden seat. The mothers would shower lavish praise on Cheetha and Chinna who had restored their pudavas to their former glory.

The pudava also needed some adept draping around the body. The gold border, the *chutty*, the parrots and lotuses had to be displayed both in front and at the back. The horizontal stripes in the middle had also to be seen on the sides. When worn in this manner, the pudava appeared beautiful. But the chest was left uncovered. A shield of various gold jewels like *kaashaali*, *poothali*, *kazhuthila*, *kettarumbu*, *thalikoottam*, *moonnizhamani*, provided the requisite cover.

My husband's family who had progressive ideas did not gift me such a pudava. I went to his illam, Nilayamgode, wearing a green silk sari brought from Madras by his elder brother's daughter Sarojini.

6 Studies

I was initiated into learning when I was four years old. As Achan was no more, it was apphan who conducted the ceremony. First, a puja was performed to propitiate Goddess Saraswathi, Lord Ganesha, and Veda Vyasa and then, alms were given to a Namboodiri. Next, apphan wrote *Harishri Ganapathaye Namah* on my tongue with a ring of gold in order to invoke the blessings of Lord Ganesha and, holding my finger, made me write the phrase on a layer of rice grains spread out in a shallow vessel called the *uruli*. In the days that followed, it was this rice, cooked, that I was given to eat. The very next day, a *brahminiamma* came to teach me the Malayalam alphabet. There was no need to summon her formally. As soon as she heard the news, unasked, she arrived with a casket of sand. Called Kuttipurathe Paappi, she must have been about fifty-five then. She was the 'writer' at the illam as it was she who taught the alphabet to all the children of Pakaravoor.

My teacher also worked at the Mukkola temple. After completing her chores there, she usually reached the illam by about ten in the morning. The northern block served as our study. She sat me down beside her, spread the sand on the floor and made me write on it. As we wrote each

* Translated by Radhika P. Menon

letter, she pronounced it loudly and asked me to repeat it after her. If I made mistakes, she would press my finger down hard, hurting me quite a lot. The fear of that pain made me very careful. The study session extended till noon and in two months, I mastered the alphabet.

Learning to read was the next step. My Valiyamma's granddaughter also studied with me. A copy of the Ramayana, which we had at the illam, was placed open before us and Paappi teacher read the lines out aloud. This went on for two months, at the end of which we completed reading the epic three times. Initiation into learning, studying the alphabet, and reading the Ramayana—this completed a girl's education. At the end of six months of studies, we gave *gurudakshina* to our teacher—two lengths of cloth and a sum of ten rupees.

Within a few months of reading the Ramayana, however, I gradually began to forget the letters of the alphabet. My interest lay in playing games in the temple compound. By the time we were seven, we started going to the temple without maidservants and did not return immediately after worship. The compound of Melekkavu was densely wooded and there was a small grassy playground in the middle, with swings made from the low-hanging creepers. There were many children of our age from the neighbouring illams. Busy with morning oblations and rituals, no one at the illam enquired about us. We played to our hearts' content and returned home only when we felt hungry.

When I turned nine, my uduthu thudangal was performed. I had to discard leaf-made loincloths and wear a cotton undergarment. An auspicious day for the ceremony had to be chosen. Consulting the almanac, Amma and Valiyamma fixed the day. Following the usual practice, an irikkanamma was sent to inform the managers of the illam about it. That very evening, they carried a huge box made of jackwood with brass fittings into the *thekke ara*, the southern room. But my box was not as grand as those of my elder sisters. After Achan's death, the show and splendour had begun to wane.

The box contained a measure of pepper and two rupees in small change over which twenty *mundu*s and four *thorthu*s were stacked. This box was mine for life and was meant to hold all my personal and private belongings. Her box was the only possession an antharjanam could claim as truly her own. After marriage, it accompanied her to her husband's house. A servant carrying the box formed the vanguard of the marriage procession. He then placed it in the thekke ara, the southern room of the groom's house.

Amma helped me wear the loincloth before a lighted lamp and prayed 'May she have plenty of food and clothes. May she enjoy marital bliss ...' and asked me to repeat it. (That was the only prayer of antharjanams in those days.) Uduthu thudangal was the first step towards womanhood and it brought tremendous changes in my daily routine. Wearing a cloth meant that it could get defiled; so a girl had to take a bath every time she touched an outsider or a person from another caste. Thus gradually, my life was confined to the inner rooms and to the company of my elder sisters. I could go to pray at the temple but not stay back to play. I could look at the boys and walk in the portico or the courtyard—only until puberty.

By then I had started to forget the alphabet. My elder sisters were however very keen on reading. But what was there to read? I am not sure whether newspapers had come to Pakaravoor then. Perhaps there was one at the pathayappura used by the Namboodiris. But it never reached us. The only available books were the ancient epics. Amma had personal copies of the *Sivapuranam*, the *Bhagavatam*, the Ramayana, and the Mahabharata. My eldest sister was greatly interested in them. In the evening, Amma usually sat in the naalukettu and read the *Bhagavatam* out loud. The other antharjanams told their beads, uttering endless prayers for a happy married life. In this atmosphere, I gradually became familiar with the ancient legends. Soon, recalling the nearly forgotten alphabet, I too began to read those books.

My Valiyettan, Neelakantan was a voracious reader. Chithrettan and Vasudevettan were no different. Parameswarettan was then a little boy. Strangely enough, there was a small library at Mookkuthala in those days. Who was in charge of it? I have no idea. Most of the books were collections of poetry by Kumaran Asan, Vallathol, and Ulloor and also translations of some Bengali novels. All my brothers had already undergone the rituals of upanayanam or *samaavarthanam* but they had never been to school. I don't know how they cultivated this habit of reading.

In the evenings they went to Koodalloor Madhom situated to the south of the Mookkuthala temple. The building was built for the Namboodiris of Koodalloor whenever they came to pray at the Mookkuthala temple. The Koodalloor Namboodiri vacated a portion of it—a small room with a veranda—to house the library. It was open for one or two hours in the evenings but very few people used it. My brothers borrowed books from this library and secretly passed them on to us. The large room in the pathayappura was my brothers' usual haunt. The books from the library were usually kept there. At dusk, after they had bathed, they came into the illam for evening prayers, concealing the books inside their mundus. There was a ritual called *chamata* for boys who had undergone the upanayanam. They conducted it by burning the twigs of chamata and it was the duty of the sisters to organize everything for the ritual. My brothers secretly left the books underneath the *aavanipalaka* they sat on. As the surrounding darkness was relieved only by the flickering flames of small oil lamps in the room, this act went unnoticed. After they left, my sisters secretly put the books into the built-in cupboard in the *vadakke ara*, northern room. Girls were not permitted to read and if the hidden books were discovered, punishment was certain. So my sisters went to the room only when there was no one in the vicinity and read behind closed doors.

The monthly rest given to menstruating girls came as a godsend to my sisters. For three days, they had to stay cooped up in a room without touching anyone. No one went in to see them either. Thus, it was possible to read uninterruptedly, without attracting any attention. Even then, there was a small problem. Touching books was taboo during those days and we lacked the courage to break the custom. But here, the servants' daughters came to our aid. One of them sat in front of us and turned the pages. Thus, we succeeded in reading books without touching them.

This was how my reading began. It was amusing to watch my sisters take such pains to read in secrecy. My eldest sister enjoyed reading the Puranas. The second eldest, Unnikkali, was more attracted to poetry. She not only read the poems of Kumaran Asan and

Ulloor, but learned them by heart as well. Even now, at eighty-one, she remembers many lines. Recently, as she lay ill, she asked me to recite *Karuna* for her. 'Listening to those lines will give me some comfort ...,' she said. And I did as I was told. To this day, she can recall the whole of *Umakeralam*.

She used to read novels as well, though they were rare and difficult to come by. It was on seeing her read translations of Bengali novels like *Durgeshanandini* and *Anandamath* that I began to take an interest in books.

Once my eldest sister wanted to learn Sanskrit. Those were the days when Achan's *gurukulam* was still functioning at the pathayappura. She had grown up hearing the mellifluous notes of clearly articulated Sanskrit *shlokas* rising from that building. So she begged Amma for permission to study the language. Although Amma repeatedly told her that girls were not supposed to learn Sanskrit, my sister was adamant. Finally, Amma managed to get Achan's permission. 'All right, we'll teach her the basics', he promised.

Achan did not have the courage to teach his daughters Sanskrit. But he had given his word to Amma. So he decided to teach my sister some of the rudiments of astrology. Perhaps he consoled himself with the thought that it might help his daughters calculate the stars of the lunar month as well as the anniversaries, without the help of the almanac.

A Nambisan was brought to the illam to teach her astrology. But something untoward happened just then. My elder sister's puberty set in. Thereafter, an antharjanam was not permitted to see strangers. How then could she study? Achan found a solution.

The teacher and the student sat in adjacent rooms so that they could not see each other and Achan sat on the doorstep in between. The teacher recited the shlokas and read the lessons loudly and my sister repeated them. Thus, the tuition went on for some months. But Achan was a very busy man. Soon it became impossible for him to find spare time. In due course, my sister's studies came to an end. They were never resumed.

Unnikkali edathi was not interested either in Sanskrit or in Kaikottikkali. Reading was her passion. I was also unconsciously drawn towards the same habit. Having almost forgotten the alphabet, initially I could read only haltingly and with many pauses. It took me several days to read books with some ease. The year was 1940–1. By then, some works of

S.K. Pottekatt, Thakazhi, and Keshava Dev were available. However, the book that attracted me the most was *Paavangal*, the Malayalam version of *Les Miserables*. My elder brother had even bought a copy of it, so I could read that novel without depending on the library and it was the book I read the most number of times. Thereafter every morning, I bowed not only before Lord Vishnu and Shiva but the Bishop of D. as well. Another novel I read several times was *Indulekha*. I think the Mookkuthala reading room did not have C.V. Raman Pillai's novels because I did not get to read any of them. Poetry did not attract me and so I did not memorize verse as my elder sister did. The other day, when she asked me to recite '*Anupama Kripanidhi*', I could not do it without a copy of the book.

By then, the atmosphere at the illam had begun to change. Two of my eldest step-brothers, who were conservative by temperament, left the illam after the partition of property. With this, my own elder brothers began to run the household. Maybe because I knew that now my wishes would be granted, I insisted on learning English, just like my elder sister had earlier wanted to study Sanskrit. At last, they gave their consent. A Nair woman called Thankam was brought from Guruvayoor and made to stay at the illam. She had passed the tenth standard and taught English, giving me lessons in history and geography as well. As I did not like mathematics, she taught me none of it.

Thankam teacher taught me for six months. Under her tutelage, I could read textbooks prescribed for the eighth standard, write addresses, and read billboards. After marriage, with this knowledge, I even read a few English novels—Pearl S. Buck's *Good Earth*, Tagore's stories, *Pride and Prejudice*, and so on. However, for some reason, this habit gradually died.

My wedding took place when I was fifteen. Thankam teacher who had stayed at the illam till then, returned to Guruvayoor and I left for my husband's house. My studies thus came to an end.

7 Visitors

Every year my second apphan, Neelakantan Namboodiri, and his two daughters visited the illam for a couple of days—festive time for us. They would be on their way back to Palakkad after participating in a literary discussion at Thrippunithura.

Neelakantan Namboodiri was a renowned Sanskrit scholar. He had spent long periods at several places including the Koodalloor gurukulam to learn Sanskrit and had also started a small gurukulam at Pakaravoor. He had his *sambandham* at the famous aristocratic Nair family of Ekkanath in Palakkad. The couple had three boys and three girls. Apphan taught all of them Sanskrit and his daughters Subhadra and Bharathi became great scholars. Every year, they participated in the literary discussion conducted by Pareekshit Thampuran at Thrippunithura and, on most occasions, won prizes.

Large illams usually had separate quarters called *madhom* to house the Nair wives of apphan Namboodiris, when they came visiting. There was a madhom at Pakaravoor too. Nair women were not permitted into the illam because they would cause a state of pollution. So they had their meals and rested in the madhom. A cook was employed exclusively to

---

* Translated by Radhika P. Menon

serve them. In those days, only women of royal lineage married to apphan Namboodiris considered it below their dignity to stay in the madhom.

After lunch, Subhadra and Bharathi usually came to the illam and sat in the northern block of rooms, vadakke ara. For us, their very presence was a source of perpetual wonderment. Subhadra was twenty and Bharathi eighteen. They had knee-length hair, wore colourful blouses, and *zari*-bordered mundus with an upper cloth, plenty of gold ornaments, and perfume as well. As they walked in, a lovely fragrance permeated the air.

It was on seeing Subhadra and Bharathi that we girls suddenly became aware of our own uncouth appearance. My elder sister was almost as old as Bharathi, but how different she looked! Her hair was not properly brushed. She didn't wear a blouse, had neither a zari-bordered mundu nor any jewellery. So she refused to enter the room and stood behind the door, trying to conceal herself as much as she could. Even I, though only six or seven years then, felt inferior, being conscious of my loincloth and lice-infested hair.

But what overwhelmed me was something else. Seated on the threshold, they lifted my younger sister and me onto their laps, and embraced and caressed us. Not yet nine and wearing no cotton loincloth, we could not be defiled by their touch! Until then, no one had touched or caressed me like that. Amma never did such a thing. The situation was the same at all illams—children were simply not fondled. Fathers very rarely saw their daughters. Conversations between them were rarer still. In fact, in those days, it was considered wrong to give special attention to one's children. Even mothers referred to their own children as 'the nephews or nieces of so and so'. Such were the times when Subhadra and Bharathi lavished their love and affection on us so openly.

When they left, they gave us a gift—a small cake of toilet soap. We had never seen such an object before. In the bath house of the illam, we had only oil, slivers of the *vaaka* bark for rubbing our bodies clean, and *thaali*, a paste made from crushed leaves that served as shampoo. None of us used soaps. So I applied the soap very sparingly and only to wash my face. What if it dissolved quickly!

Nor did I ever brush my hair because there was no such thing as a comb at the illam. And most of us had plenty of lice in our hair. The mirror too was a thing of sheer wonder. I was six years old when I saw a small mirror that a bookseller brought to the illam. He was one of the very few vendors who came calling. He wore a checked mundu at the waist and wrapped a thorthu around the head. Squatting just outside the portico of the manager's building, he displayed his wares—volumes on *Vaakya, Manipravalam, Jnanapana, Sheelavati,* and the like. Only children were allowed to see him. I enjoyed picking out various objects, one by one from his box and taking them inside for Amma and my elder sisters to see. Amma would buy religious books for my sisters. It was only after a lot of pleading and sulking that I got Amma's permission to buy a mirror which I treasured for a long time.

Another object in that man's box was a polish for cleaning bronze bangles. The antharjanams and girls of illams, however prosperous, wore only bronze bangles because gold was not allowed. But their designs differed according to the financial status of the household—rich women sported rounded bangles while the rest had flat ones. We needed polish to keep them clean and bright. Those who could not afford it wore dull bangles.

Another visitor to the illam was K.P. Namboodiri—Kolathappalli Pothayan Namboodiri. He had studied at the Sanskrit gurukulam of the illam for some time. Later he became the owner of the famous K.P. Namboodiri's Tooth Powder. But, at that time, he had not started the business on a large scale. He visited the illam on special occasions and also attended the festival of *vaaram* at Mukkolakkavu. He walked all the way from Vanneri, crossing the Naranippuzha by ferry. His cloth bag bulged with leaf-packets containing tooth powder. The packets were pegged at various prices—one *mukkaal,* two mukkaals, one *ana,* and so on—depending on the quantity of the powder contained. To the buyers, he gave a free printed leaflet which carried a song, penned by him, elaborating the virtues of his product.

As we were children, we could go to see K.P. Namboodiri. Once, we bought a couple of those packets with the money we pestered out of Amma and got two song books from him. Before long, we learnt the poems by heart. We carefully put away the packets and used the powder only sparingly. However, we recited the poems regularly. Like the soap and the mirror, the tooth powder too was a wonderful fancy item.

The priest of Mookkuthala Melekkavu gave us each a special stone collected from a small pit near the Devi temple. It was set in gold and tied round the neck of a child during the rice-giving ceremony and removed only on her wedding day. I wore a chain that carried three such stones as amulets along with seeds like *ilanjikkuru* and *kadukka*. Besides, there was a silver amulet in my waistband. These and the bronze bangles were my usual ornaments. Gold jewellery—like *kuzhalumothiram, palakkamothiram*, and gold amulet in the waistband—was allowed only on special days. On such occasions, we had to mark our forehead with a *tilak* of sandal-paste. Later on, *bindi*s made of burnt rice powder became fashionable. By afternoon, we wiped off the sandal tilak and put on the homemade bindi. Rice grains were roasted till they turned dark, ground into a thick paste, mixed with oil, and stored in bottles to make the glossy black bindis all of us liked. *Kanmashi* or kohl was used to adorn the eyes.

After all this make-up, we considered ourselves beautiful. In those days, to be small built, light skinned, and to have thick hair were signs of beauty. The prospect of having tall daughters terrified Amma.

My elder sisters were very tall. When one of them was given away in marriage, her height became a topic of discussion and there were comments like 'Now we won't need a ladder to take firewood from the kitchen-loft'. The scorn must have hurt Amma deeply.

'If only one of them was of average height,' Amma would say fervently, almost like a prayer. And as if to prevent me from shooting up, she occasionally held my shoulders and pressed them down. Her wishes were fulfilled and I did not grow tall.

However, Subhadra and Bharathi conquered our hearts by setting new aesthetic standards. One of our daily prayers was 'If there is another birth, may it be in Ekkanath House'.

8 Journey

I went to Mookkuthala temple recently because writer and actor V.K. Sriraman had asked me to go there for a film shooting. Mookkuthala temple is associated with my childhood. I was born and brought up in its vicinity and Sriraman wanted me to recount my childhood experiences against the backdrop of the temple. Thus, I got an opportunity to journey back into my past once more.

Mookkuthala temple is beautiful. Its walls enclose an area of about seven acres of wooded land. In my childhood, too, the woods were as dense. But today, they appeared even more beautiful. The *vazha*, a rarely seen tree believed to be sacred to the Bhagawathi, grew there in large numbers. Some two thousand of these were to be found in that compound. Women wore its leaves in their hair as tokens of the deity's blessing. *Antharjanams* kept these pressed between the slats of their palm leaf umbrellas which they carried as a protective shield. Babies were customarily taken outdoors only after their *choroonu* ceremony when they tasted rice for the first time and then their mothers held an extra vazha leaf in their hands for the infant's safety. The low-slung creepers which connected the trees with each other served as a swing and gave us immense pleasure in our childhood days.

* Translated by Indira Menon

Years later, once again, I sat on these creepers to revive memories of my past for the camera.

The temple walls enclosing the dense woods are higher than was prevalent at the time. My *apphan* from Pakaravoor had built it. That wall did not seem as high this time perhaps because mud had been piled on the surrounding roads to raise their level. In the olden days, there were no roads near the temple, only deep and narrow dirt tracks. Mookkuthala had no streets, just a rough-hewn trail from Shankarakulam to Naranipuzha. Kannaenkavu, Kizhekavu, Melekavu, the Pakaravoor Shiva temple were all connected by such pathways. On either side, there were high thorn fences and some thorns always lay scattered on the ground. Since none of us had any footwear, they pierced our feet and taking them out was a daily routine. Some had a knack for removing them painlessly. Today there are no lanes, only tarred roads. Many cars and autorickshaws run on them and people can now be set down at the entrance to the temple.

Sriraman, too, had asked me to do this. '*Ammamma*, please hire a car to come here.' Therefore, I travelled alone in a car from Tirur near Trichur to Mookkuthala some forty kilometres away and arrived at the temple.

Between the ages of six and eleven, I spent the best part of the day among these trees around the temple. At seven in the morning we, a group of children from Pakaravoor, would arrive there to pray. The antharjanams and the children from the neighbouring Namboodiri houses, the *illams*, would accompany us. It was compulsory for all of us to pray at the temple every morning. We could go home immediately after that for our morning meal. But we children stayed on, swinging on the creepers and playing hide and seek among the trees till ten or eleven in the morning. After breakfast, by about eleven o'clock, we'd be back in the temple where some special function was held almost every day. The children and the Namboodiris stayed on for lunch, though the antharjanams could not. In the evening, it was back again to the temple after a bath and there were more games till nightfall. We often sat down to listen to *vaaram*, the chanting of Vedas—a tradition specific to the Namboodiris—followed by dinner. Afterwards, the children returned home by seven or eight o'clock, walking behind a group of Namboodiris who carried lanterns, either glass-covered lanterns or stone lanterns. The former consisted of a trivet with a wick, lit with coconut oil, and placed inside a glass. This glass had a tin lid, a chain, and a hook to be dangled on a finger as they walked. The stone lantern was more modern. It had a thick iron square-shaped cage, thick glass, a door at the side, and a strong handle at the top. This door had to be opened to light the wick set in a trivet and placed in a small plate containing oil. (Kerosene oil was not permitted within the temple premises.) The lanterns shed only a dim light which the children followed to reach home. Thus, for us, a group of twenty-odd girls, the forests around the temple became our playground for the best part of the day.

There were so many kinds of trees in the dense woods! *Kotta, ayani, naval, ungu, vazha, ilanji*—all growing so tall, reaching skyward. The creepers around one tree intertwined with the next and leaves about a foot deep lay scattered below. The numerous birds among the trees ensured that birdsong always resounded in the forest. Though it was cool and green, nobody had seen snakes there. The large number of monkeys found there at one time had been taken away by the monkey catchers who doped them, shut them up in cages, and let them loose beyond the river Bharathapuzha in Kuttippuram. In the rainy season, they carried these cages in river rafts and released them in the forests on the other side of the river. Nobody harmed the monkeys found within the temple complex. Feeding them sweet *payasam* was a part of the offering to the deity. Expectant women would go to Mookkuthala temple in their eighth month of pregnancy and offer payasam to the Goddess. This was served on strips of banana leaves placed in a row and fed to the monkeys afterwards.

There was a *kokkarani* in the middle of the forest. (Kokkarani was a well that was not quite a water tank.) The water was as cool as dew drops and its surface was still and unruffled. In the olden days, monkeys would smear themselves with the slush and mud in the well.

We children performed a Devi puja on special days. The antharjanams and the young girls together went round the sanctum of the temple seven times which constituted one round, with twelve such rounds to be completed. This was referred to as *panthrandu vekkal*, taking twelve turns. We'd hold a vazha leaf in our hands when we took the rounds. We'd pierce the leaf once at the end of each round. After we pierced it seven times, we'd change this leaf for a fresh one. Thus, we'd have twelve leaves in our hands signifying the completion of eighty-four rounds, or twelve turns.

But the children could not complete this in the morning. The remaining rounds would then have to be done in the evening. Sometimes, in the midst of this we would go into the forest, wash our faces in the cold waters of the kokkarani, swing for a while on the creepers, eat some fruit of the kotta and naval trees, and then return to continue our rounds with renewed vigour.

It seemed that walking was central to people's lives in those days. Everyone walked to the temple, as also to other places. There were few roads. There was only a narrow dirt road going past the *pathayappura* that housed the granary as well as assembling spaces for Namboodiris, through Changaramkulam to Naranipuzha. Buses did not drive on this stretch and we had to go to Edappal or Chalissery to board a bus. Nobody wanted to own a car in Pakaravoor though it was not for lack of funds to buy them. The only car we saw was Payyapalli Vappu's white one. We would marvel at it from a distance as it drove past on the road raising dust.

In our childhood, we had not travelled by car. Travelling by bus too was a rare occurrence. In general we did not move out of Mookkuthala. We were not sent to school either. The only reason we were allowed to go to the Kannenkavu Temple *pooram* festival was because it was held near Mookkuthala. In those days aristocratic homes staged Kathakali dances on their premises. But the people of Mookkuthala were not interested in Kathakali. We journeyed only from our illam to the temple and back, and this daily walk constituted the world of our wanderings.

Our annual journey on foot to the *ammathu* was the equivalent of a jaunt to a foreign land. Ammathu was the illam in which Amma was born and where she grew up. This was called *Naripatta mana*, situated in Karalmanna, 50 kilometres away from Mookkuthala. Every year, Amma, her daughters and an *irikkanamma* made this trip. The sons were not a part of this group as boys were required to pray at the Mookkuthala Bhagawati temple without break for a period of twelve years.

This journey was undertaken at the beginning of summer, depending on when the water level in the river went down. But we always found that we needed a boat to cross the river at Pattambi. In those days, the boatmen did not pull up their boats ashore and leave them there, because the forests were dense with trees and the rivers were full of water.

Much preparation had to be made for the journey. Amma would make a bundle of the clothes for use in the four or five days at her family home. We girls did not need any clothes. A few strips of tender arecanut spathes were packed to serve as undergarments because Karalmanna and the surrounding areas did not have arecanut trees. On the journey too, we girls wore only these. But since we were travelling, we would tie a gold amulet strung on a white thread around the waist. Though our bodies were left uncovered, our heads were not. We'd fold a towel in half and wrap it round our heads. Amma would pleat a cloth *mundu* and tie it around her waist, use another to cover her whole body and take an umbrella to prepare for the journey. She would carry four or five rupees rolled up in a corner of the mundu. The money for the travel would be entrusted to the irikkanamma since tendering the bus fare was her responsibility.

Amma had a narrative about the five rupees that she carried on the journey. This money was not given by the family. It was not as if the family did not have the money but it was not customary in those days to give any to the antharjanam even for her smallest needs. Tradition decreed that they find their own money to meet their special expenses. Amma had saved these four or five rupees from the *pidiyari*, a fistful of rice.

Each morning, Neelakantan Nambisan, who was in charge of the kitchen provisions would measure out the daily requirements and place them near the kitchen door. A larger quantity of rice than was necessary was always doled out because of the number of people to be fed and the several passers-by who arrived unexpectedly for a meal. When Nambisan measured out the rice, Amma would take a small quantity from it and put it away in her personal container in the kitchen. When the container was full, she would give it to a maidservant to be sold outside. You required several *kudanna* of rice to earn one or one and a half rupees. After making five rupees in this way, Amma would gather the courage to set out for her ammathu. In other places too, the women of aristocratic families of the time saved money in this manner for even their most pressing needs. In less prosperous families, even this facility was denied to them.

After our customary bath and prayer, we'd eat hot rice before setting out on our journey. Amma would not eat anything but the irikkanamma would have consumed the previous day's gruel. Amma would carry a small umbrella with a short handle made especially for use during travel. The irikkanamma would be an elderly woman dressed in a cloth tied around her waist as an undergarment over which she draped another mundu with a towel thrown across her shoulder.

We'd walk straight to Chalissery, five miles away, cutting across Chiyyanur fields which were four miles wide, moving towards the east to the Chalissery marketplace. By about eleven in the morning we'd reach a middle class illam called Palakkattiri, where we'd first have a bath. The lunch of curry, vegetable, pickle, and watery buttermilk tasted delicious because we were always ravenously hungry when we reached there. All the other wayfarers, irrespective of their numbers, would be fed by them. This was the practice followed in most illams—they were happy to feed all those who went there.

After lunch, we set out for the Guruvayoor-Pattambi road nearby to take the bus. There was usually a long wait involved and, even when the bus did come, there was no certainty that they would take the antharjanam on board. The reason was that she was saddled with a palm-leaf umbrella which would cause discomfort to other passengers.

In those days, the buses that plied on this route belonged to a rich man from Ponnani, Murugan Ravunni Nair. This was at first called 'Shastha Service' and was later changed to 'Murugan Service'. When the bus arrived, we'd climb in and sit right at the back. My younger sister and I would get on first, followed by Amma and the companion.

The bus was run on charcoal. A large drum was placed at the rear end of the bus near the last seats and the coal smouldered in it, filling the interior with smoke and coal-dust. All the fair-skinned children would look black when they alighted. The bus conductor would take Amma's umbrella away and, going around the bus, hand it back to her from outside. Amma would sit in a corner all wrapped up, holding tightly on to the umbrella's handle so it wouldn't fly away. We, with our arecanut loin-cloth and our heads covered, would crouch as far away from the smouldering drum as we could in order not to touch it, even inadvertently, and be singed. Still, that journey was an exciting one. Houses and trees appeared to fly backwards at great speed. We'd sit there with our hearts filled with joy praying that this bus journey would go on for a while longer. At last, the bus would reach Pattambi and we had to get down at the riverfront.

Though it was summer, the river was not dry. More often than not, a boat was readily available otherwise we'd have to wait for it to come back from the other bank. After the crossing, we'd duck into the water and run and play on the sand. We'd dry ourselves with the towel round our heads. We liked to bathe in the sandy areas rather than use the built-up steps and we'd swim till sundown. By the side of the river, there was an *oottuppura*—a dining hall built for Brahmins and run by one. We learnt

afterwards that his name was Chidambaranathan. Though there was also a
hotel at that time in Pattambi, this oottuppura was used by those Brahmins
who were either disinclined or too poor to go there. Uncooked rice was
distributed there and people could take it to the river, wash themselves
and the rice, and fill the vessel with river water. On their return, they'd
find the firewood and the fireplace ready for cooking. Salt, chillies, and
tamarind, were available, also free of cost, in the kitchen. After dinner, the
hall could be used for sleeping.

We did not use this dining space. Amma would choose an isolated spot
outside the hall on the veranda and sit there all wrapped up, holding her
umbrella. We'd sit apart, not touching her in order not to pollute her.
The irikkanamma would dole out the beaten-rice and bananas from the
bundle, which we'd wash down with river water. Then we'd set out again
to take the bus for Cheruplasseri.

When we reached our destination after so much hardship, our grandmother ammamma, did not seem too pleased to see us. It may be that
she did not show the joy that she felt inside. The Namboodiri families of
the period were very particular about this. There was to be no display of
any emotion, particularly affection—a convention strictly adhered to at
the time.

We'd stay for four days at ammamma's. This illam was situated on the
banks of the Thootha puzha, which never ran dry. The river was our friend.
On the fifth day, our return journey would begin early in the morning in
the same manner and we'd reach Pakaravoor only after sunset.

Yet another annual trip was the
one made to Guruvayoor. The difference here was that we didn't have
to walk to Chalissery—instead, we
went by boat from the Pakaravoor
landing. All around the Pakaravoor
jetty were the back-waters and low-ly-
ing water-filled rice fields. Water lilies
bloomed in them. We'd pluck these
with both hands and fill the boat only
to be scolded by the boatman when
the boat tilted to a side. In summer,
the water level was low and the boat

would climb on to the ridged edges of the fields. Then the boatman had to get down and push the boat away from the land. This added task had to be performed many times till we reached Kattakambal (known locally as Kattambala) landing. Near this landing was the Perumballi illam which welcomed all the passers-by, however numerous, with great affection. They were an aristocratic, prosperous family. After lunch, we'd return to the marketplace to wait for the Nambiar Service charcoal bus.

In earlier times, Amma used to walk to Guruvayoor. But in my childhood days, the Nambiar Bus service started plying right up to the western entrance, *padinjare nada*, of the temple.

We stayed in a madhom run by Pakaravoor and cooked the rice we had carried with us. Next day, when Amma was busy appealing to the deity, our attention would stray to the display of fancy things in the shops at the western entrance. After making the customary offerings, Amma would give us four anas from the remaining money. With this, we'd buy the song book on Sheelavati, a polish with which to shine our bell-metal bangles, a bamboo flute for three quarters of an ana, and return satisfied that we had fulfilled all our desires.

When I grew up and attained maturity, all these journeys stopped. I was not permitted to go even to the temple. The only place I was allowed out was to the kitchen-tank in the compound. With all excursions stopped, I retreated into my illam like a bird with clipped wings. Till I left home after my wedding two years later, I could catch glimpses of the sky only on my trips to this kitchen-tank.

As I sat near the Mookkuthala temple with the imposing trees around me, my childhood excursions remained integral to my remembrance of the past. The film shooting which evoked these memories did not take long. I rode back home alone to 'Kapilavastu' in my taxi, the joyous recollections of my early journeys lingering in my mind.

9 A Group Dance

Onam season saw us children and women eagerly waiting for a visitor—Pattikkattu Kunhikuttyamma from Kallorma village, east of Mookkuthala. On Thiruvonam day, we ate an early lunch and held our breath waiting for her arrival, our eyes scanning the narrow path running between the eastern fields, the *kizhakke paadam*. She was our Kaikottikkali instructor and we could begin only after she arrived.

She must have been fifty-five years old at the time though she did not look it. Her height was just right and she was slim without being skinny. Fair skinned and luxuriant hair tied up at the side of her head, the vestiges of her youthful beauty were still visible. The jewellery she sported—large earrings, a chain as well as a broad necklace, rings on her fingers—sparkled in the sunlight and announced her arrival from a distance. Around her waist, she tied a wide-bordered cloth undergarment under a *mundu* with a narrow gold border, and the upper half of her body was covered with a blouse and another mundu. The transparent gold-bordered mundu did not hide the black-lined edges of the under-cloth. This was considered stylish at that time and the song she had composed for our group dance made specific references to such bordered undergarments. She brought a change of clothes with her and stayed with us for a couple of days. In some

* Translated by Indira Menon

ways, she was considered a special guest. She used the rear entrance to the house but, even before her arrival, a mat would be spread in a room at the back for her to rest after her post-lunch, two-mile walk in the afternoon sun. But she was so excited at the prospect of the dance that she forgot her weariness, and was ready to begin as soon as her perspiration had dried and she had relaxed a little.

During Onam season, celebrations in Pakaravoor included four days of Kaikottikkali, the only art form known to the *antharjanams* who were eager to display their dancing prowess. On a smaller scale, this dance was performed when the bride was brought to the husband's home for the first time. But there was nothing to equal Kaikottikkali during Onam: that was the real thing! In addition to the antharjanams, other castes like the Ambalavasis, the Nair women who worked in the *illam* as well as from Nair families outside, participated in this dance. They would start at about half-past eleven in the morning and go on till late in the evening, till about seven or eight o'clock. Those who arrived in the bright afternoon sunshine returned in the dark carrying lighted flares.

Melekkavu, the Bhagavathi temple, was situated in the centre of Mookkuthala village surrounded by forests. Just outside the temple compound were the residences of the temple employees, known as '*pushpakam*'. The outer row housed the Namboodiris; and the Warrier and Nair residences were in the middle. At a time when a visit to the temple was central to daily living, any interaction between the antharjanams and the other women took place, if at all, only on the temple premises. There they decided the venue of each year's Kaikottikkali, usually opting for homes with adolescent girls, which was how Pakaravoor came to host Kaikottikkali continuously for many years.

In the more prosperous illams and Nair homes, young girls were taught this dance by in-house Kaikottikkali instructors. If the number of children in the family was inadequate to form a circle, those from neighbouring houses were co-opted. Ammalu Amma who taught me music and dance had formed a group with the daughters of the women companions of the family. Thus, for Onam celebrations, the instructor brought along her group to the illam.

Kaikottikkali was performed on the four days succeeding Thiruvonam day. Lunch was early on Onam day, it being compulsory to eat at home on that occasion. After lunch, all the women hurried towards the venue of Onakkali. Not all of them participated in the dance and songs; many were merely onlookers. Old or young, no woman stayed back at home after lunch on those four days. By the time we had eaten, women stood clamouring at the back door to be allowed inside.

The dance was held in the hall where we ate lunch. After the used leaves were removed and the floor cleaned, the women literally flowed in. The main doors to the hall were closed when we danced because most of the participants were antharjanams who could neither see nor be seen by any man other than a family member. Nair women were unhappy at this because they believed that the presence of men in the audience added glamour to the dance. Therefore on the fourth day, the venue was shifted to a Nair family's courtyard where a thatched shed was temporarily erected for the purpose. Naturally, only Nair women participated in this but the sounds were audible even from a distance. On that day, the antharjanams held merely a token dance performance before going their separate ways.

A member of the family where Kaikottikkali was held, started the proceedings by dancing to a song praising Ganapathi. This was followed by the praise of Saraswathi, the Goddess of Learning. Then it was time to invite the graceful dancers to perform, with a song praising their beauty, their pleasing ways, and comparing their speech to a parrot's. These dancers were familiar with many songs which did not necessarily constitute a part of a narrative, like the rendering of 'How do you submit to this, Yashoda?' considered to be well suited to this dance form. Everyone also enjoyed the one praising Yashoda's beauty. Pride of place was given to songs which had four, eight, or fourteen *vritham*. We danced to Damayanthi's lament in Nala's story set to music, 'Deserted in the forest'; and to our musical rendition of Harishchandra's verse-drama 'O, Remover of affliction ... Lord of the Universe, bless us so we can repay Kaushikan's debt'. Though we sang the songs from *Nala Charitham* and other stories set to tune, it was difficult for the chorus to take it up. So we quickly moved to more popular songs, especially to those which combined religious and erotic sentiments.

The dance which was leisurely at first with the tune spun out to suit slow-paced movements, changed mid-way to high speed energy, responding with passion to the acceleration of the lilt whether it was *kummi*,

kurathi, vanchipattu, anchadipattu, or *porvilipattu.* The circle divided into
two groups—one as Parvathi's followers and the other as Lakshmi's, each
ridiculing the other's husband. The spirited song about '*The flower maiden
and the divine Lakshmi*' amused the dancers and their audience with its
witty references. In 'porvilipattu', too, the group split into two sections.
The terms used in Kathakali—when one character challenged the other
to a fight—were adopted here as well. Some of the lines describing the
opponent as 'wicked and vicious', 'stubborn and unfaithful', hailing him
contemptuously 'hey, you!' were sung to the accompaniment of resounding dance steps. The response was made by the opposing group in the same
beat and speed as the challenger. Thus, the verbal assault and counter-
offensive, beat and dance and noise, and the oil lamps in the room burning
more visibly after sunset, transformed Onakkali into a celebration.

Kunhikuttyamma's arrival enthused everyone. She stood in the centre
of the group like an instructor and corrected and scolded anyone who
made a mistake in the step or in the beat. She always began with her own
composition:

The dance of the doe-eyed maidens
Brings Thiruvonam here.
These doe-eyed girls
Dance their Onakkali, unseen

was how it began.

An interlined bordered undercloth,
A gold-edged cloth over it,
Strutting along, in blouses,
Everyone stands amazed.
Ensnaring bangles
And rings on all fingers
Necklaces too and chains,
Everyone stands amazed.

This was about their dress and the confidence they exhibited in their
appearance.

The singers imparted the heady nature of feminine beauty and its effect
on the men to the dancers and their onlookers.

Fragrant all over
And the spreading fragrance,

Held the men in thrall,
Marvelling at the maidens.
Don't miss a beat,
Don't falter when you bend,
Never be complacent,
Nor demure, O maidens.

The emphasis was on the amatory nature of the dance. The song ended with a description of the *devas* lining up in the skies, forsaking their semi-divine women to admire the beautiful girls dancing the Onakkali.

Kunhikuttyamma was adept at sinking to floor level as she danced without missing a beat. The gestures and eroticism of Mohiniattam which she brought to her performance were enjoyed by the audience. Her movements reflected the import of the words. She sang some verses with added passion and the onlookers took up the chorus with equal vigour. Then Kunkikuttyamma's excitement mounted further and her dance became frenzied. This was her cue to move away from the centre towards the sides, to force the dancers with a little downward push to sink lower and to threaten to slap those who missed a beat—all this without losing a step herself. By the time the song ended, she was tired and needed to rest for a while in a corner before resuming the performance.

About fifty to a hundred women participated in the dance, each in her best clothes. The Nair women who came from elsewhere wore gold-bordered *mundus* and blouse. The antharjanams did not wear blouses. They pleated and draped a set of two matching mundus which was called the '*pudava*'. This was readied for the occasion—washed, starched, and the broad gilt edge brightened by rubbing a mixture of a coloured powder and the flower of the *plashu* tree on it. The ornaments they wore like *kaashaali* and *poothaali* hung on their chests like a coat of armour and were considered beautiful. On the fourth day of the dance held in the open in a Nair *tharavad*, men were present to appreciate their efforts with cries of 'Well done!' But the antharjanams who danced behind closed doors had no men in their audience to cheer them.

Kaikottikkali in the Onam season was danced in two parts. In the first phase, when songs of praise and other slow tunes were sung, Antharjanams danced apart from others. If they were defiled by physical contact with other dancers, they were not allowed even a drink of water. At three o'clock, they went into the kitchen, ate papadams, fried banana chips and ripe bananas, drank some water, and started the second phase of the dance. This involved standing together and tapping the partner's palms rhythmically. It was then that the dance acquired grandeur and became a general celebration. The stage rejected all segregation and restored parity in the unified performances.

Kunhikuttyamma was always at hand to support and encourage the dancers, taking only short spells of rest to recharge herself. She not only danced to her songs but also effectively emoted the feelings expressed in them. When she sang '*All the men swooned ...*' , she enacted the scene. It seemed as if the devas had actually appeared in the sky, judging by the excitement on her face. Perhaps it was because she was eager for the devas and the menfolk to applaud her performance that she wanted the fourth day's dance to be shifted to an open space.

In her youth, Kunhikuttyamma was considered to have been a coquette. She was the wife of a well-respected person in the community who gave her everything she asked for and treated her royally. In her heyday, she used to go to the Mookkuthala temple in a bullock-cart, decked in shimmering blouses and several ornaments, accompanied by her *irikkanammas*. Her husband died suddenly and she had no children. Even at that time, it was not uncommon for Nair women to re-marry, but she did not, though she had fallen on bad days after her husband's death. During her prosperous period, she had not gone out to other houses to perform Kaikottikkali. But now that she did, her confidence in her beauty which many men had admired and which she still retained, and her indifference to other people's opinion, showed in her attitude. Once, as she sat down on a mat in the room at the northern corner of our house, the *vadakkini*, she said, 'I am not among those who should be relegated to this space in the *illam*. In my house I used to sleep on a teak bed with seven mattresses on it.'

On all three days of Onam celebrations, the dance ended only after dark. Many antharjanams had small children and old people waiting for them at home. But nobody complained. The irikkanammas in the illam readied the flares which they lit at the lamp burning in the hall to help them make their way in the dark. We, the members of the family, moved towards the tank for a bath in the dim light of a lamp at the end of a road saying as we went, '*Naaley*'—till tomorrow—determined to have a more spirited dance the next day.

Kunhikuttyamma stayed back and regaled us with songs and stories of Unniarcha and Kungi. The moral was that women should never consider themselves inferior to men, but must learn to stand up for themselves like Unniarcha did. We marvelled at these tales of courage, but Amma disapproved of them. She took us aside and advised us, 'She may sing and dance well, but her comments are unwarranted and not worthy of emulation'.

After marriage, I missed all the excitement and joy of Onakkali because Chathanoor did not have the same closely-knit society as Mookkuthala. There was no temple nearby and therefore no bi-daily congregation; there were no immediate neighbours either. We met each other only at weddings. It was impossible to form close bonds during such casual contacts. After a while, I did not miss Kaikottikkali in the Onam season because I was steered towards the Nilayamgode family's involvement in societal reforms. Kunhikuttyamma also faded from my mind except as a dim picture in my memory.

Years later, when I visited valiyettan in Mookkuthala, I came across an extraordinarily well-crafted teak bed with beautiful carvings on it. I was told that it had originally been adorned with a silk canopy edged with mercury-filled glass balls and a 'pankha' usually found only on royal beds. The 'pankha' was tied to a cloth rope and connected to an adjoining room where a servant sat and pulled the rope all night so that his master could have uninterrupted sleep.

I was curious to find out whom the bed had belonged to earlier.

'I got it for about eighty rupees from a woman who insisted I buy it off her. She had seen better times but had fallen on bad days, dogged by disease and poverty.' Before I could ask for more details, my sister said: 'You remember Pattikattu Kunhikutty who used to come here during Onam time to dance Kaikottikkali? She was the one who insisted we buy the bed.'

I stood still, marvelling at the end of a story symbolized by the dismantled decorations on a regal bed, remembering the extraordinary woman who had slept on it.

10 *Sheelavati*

In my childhood I used to recite songs and jingles memorized by listening to others. The best known of these were the lines from *Sheelavati*.

Sheelavati was a slim booklet of about eight or ten pages without even an outer cover, written by an unknown author. This was used by our mothers to mark the pages of the *Ramayana, Bhagavatham*, and *Mahabharatham* which they read in the afternoons.

The poor quality paper, the lack of an outer cover, and constant use, caused the booklet to disintegrate very quickly. Then it was replaced by a new copy which cost only three-quarters of an ana. Every year when we went to Guruvayoor via Kattambala, we bought more copies of this booklet.

The bookseller who came to the *illam* occasionally would, in addition to this, bring bound books such as *SriKrishna Charitham*, *Manipravalam*, and *Vadakkanpattu* which did not fall apart easily. Therefore, *Sheelavati* was the most sought after by us. But the maidservants preferred songs celebrating Unniarcha and Palattu Koman which we too would have liked to possess except that our mothers believed that these tales were a bad influence on young minds.

* Translated by Indira Menon

My second elder sister Unikkali loved poetry and could recite *SriKrishna Charitham* and *Manipravalam* which she had memorized, unlike my older sister and I and the others who could sing only the songs from *Sheelavati*. These filled our hearts and rose to our lips with our mothers' encouragement. They believed that reciting it was good for us.

Sheelavati was born into a wealthy family but was forced to marry an ascetic Ugrathapas, an old leper, in deference to her father's wishes. She lived in a forest and devoted her time to nursing her husband. I remember the lines narrated thus.

Rising at dawn, bathing in the brook
Back home without delay
Husking the finest paddy into
Choicest rice, cooking it just right,
making a dish with peas, she prepared
A perfect meal. Milking a goat
She boiled the milk, and mixing
It with the rice, she lovingly fed (her husband)

Softly rubbing the sores with the lather
Of incha, she made them clean and clear ...

Nothing that she did to nurse him, clean, bathe, and feed him met with his approval. He had only criticism to offer.

She, always a dutiful nurse,
Nurtured and indulged a wrathful man.
Heart full of anger, mind filled with rancour,
The ascetic let loose his barbs.
Woman! Your deceitful face
Is to me an unpleasant sight,
The food you serve
Lacks taste and salt,
Fit only for the garbage bin.
How can I eat such uneatable food
Cooked and served with such indifference?
So be aware you're not my saviour,
You cannot save me, Sheelavati.

Sheelavati ate only her husband's leftovers. On one occasion, she found her leper husband's severed finger in his half-eaten food. She showed no disgust but just moved it aside and ate the rest of the food.

One day, Ugrathapas ordered her to take him to a prostitute. That was the first time she dared to offer him any advice.

O, virtuous husband of mine,
O ascetic and master of mine,
O remember that only harm can befall
The company of fallen women.

But the advice did not deter Ugrathapas. He refused to listen to her and Sheelavati was forced to carry him to a prostitute.

On the way, she inadvertently stepped on the foot of an ascetic in deep meditation when she tried to avoid walking into a ditch full of dirty water. The ascetic, whose concentration was disturbed, cursed Sheelavati that she'd be a widow before the next day's sunrise.

This curse upset Sheelavati greatly. She put her husband down and commenced a grim meditation to ensure that the sun did not rise the next day. As a result, the sun did not rise and the universe came to a standstill. At last, the devas relented, appeared before Sheelavati, and gave her husband the boon of youth and good health.

This was Sheelavati's story. I don't know if my brothers had heard this tale. But we girls knew this by heart and we sang the lines as we went along.

But when we played games such as *kallukali* and *vattukali*, we heard a different set of songs. Our mothers' *irikkanammas* had daughters who were our playmates. Their tunes were not like the *Sheelavati* songs that we always hummed. One of these was the story of Unniarcha.

Unniarcha of Attumanamel house
Lay down to sleep after her meal.

In this song, Unniarcha had no time to nurse her husband like Sheelavati did. Against his wishes, she was on her way to the Allimalar Kavu to watch the dance and hear the discourses at the temple there. On the way, she was stopped at Nadapurathangadi by a group of Muslims. She advanced, roaring a challenge, and the men were paralysed with fear. These were the stories that our friends sang to us from the song book of Unniarcha their mothers had bought from the itinerant book seller. When we hummed the tale of Sheelavati's care of her husband in a low tone, these girls sang of the various exploits in *Vadakkangatha* books with great enthusiasm.

Gradually, the words seeped into my subconscious and, as I moved about inside the house or the kitchen or walked towards the tank, I too started humming these rather than the lines from *Sheelavati*. But I was soon dissuaded from my musical efforts by Amma who tried to explain that singing these verses did not befit the daughters of the house.

Recently, when I met my second elder sister, she sang the old *Sheelavati* song once again. She also gave me a part of *Thacholi Chandu*, a book she had bought sometime later. It seems that I was not the only one who had been attracted to the forbidden tales.

Times had changed when I moved to Nilayamgode after my wedding. I, too, had read some other books in the meantime, like *Pavangal* and *Chinthavishtayaya Sita*. But everyone's favourite book was Changanpuzha's *Ramanan*. Even the antharjanams were fascinated by his poetry. We were no longer interested in *Sheelavati's* travails but knew Ramanan's tale by heart.

The servant maids in Nilayamgode were young women who did not care for such reading. They were enthralled by books like *Sarojini Kuttyyude Kadunkai* and *Kavalappara Komban*. I still remember one of them finishing the former and breaking into uncontrollable sobs.

11 Floods

The Mookkuthala region was bounded on three sides by backwaters commonly known in the past as *kadavu*, the landing place. To the east was Srayi kadavu, the south Uppungal kadavu, and the west Narani kadavu. The landlocked north led to the areas around Edappal and Chalissery. But travel in any other direction was possible only by boat. The more aristocratic and wealthy *illam*s and *tharavad*s had their own boats and they employed one or two people with the specific responsibility of rowing them. Transporting sheaves of corn and hay after harvest from distant areas reclaimed from the backwaters and carrying coconuts plucked from plantations would have been impossible without boats. The fact that this was the landing place for boats may have been the reason why it was called kadavu.

The waters had to be drained to sow the seeds for *punja* cultivation. First a bund was constructed to which the waters were diverted through a narrow canal by rotating wheels. There would be twenty to thirty such wheels in a row near the bund. Day and night, labourers would take turns working the wheels with their feet to haul the water into the bund. This was usually done in the month of Thulaam. They would sing continuously to ward off boredom and fatigue. But, though they sang through

* Translated by Indira Menon

the day and night, we children could hear them clearly only at night. The songs were about the exploits of Palattu Koman and other such heroes. On Thulaam nights we would fall asleep to these songs which seemed to come floating towards us from a distance; and if we woke up at night, these notes of music would still be faintly audible.

By the time I was seven years old, these strains had faded away almost totally because the wheels had begun to be replaced by huge engines in the backwaters. We had watched this machinery being transported with a sense of awe from the stories told about it. That year, a large platform of bamboo was raised in the watery expanse. A whole bamboo forest must have gone into building such a platform. The bamboos were brought in bullock carts and taken midstream by boats. Fully grown bamboos were cut to the same length and hammered down into the waterbed where the waters rose just above the waist. These were fixed side by side in a row to the required width and palm leaves woven together were tied firmly around them. This would then appear like a huge receptacle made of bamboo and palm leaves. Soil obtained from levelling mounds in the forest areas was transported by boats and used to fill them to the top where they appeared to be ten to fifteen cents wide. The mud was evened out to align with the bamboos and flattened by laying wooden boards on its surface. The platform was then ready for the engine to be placed on it.

Eight or ten boats were tied together and planed timber was laid on top for the machinery to rest upon, for transportation to the structure from Kattambala kadavu. Each one of these was of forty horsepower (as we learnt later) and was the equivalent of twenty or thirty wheels. Large numbers of people were required to transfer the engine from the boats to the platform. Philippose from Tiruvalla was the first to bring the possible uses of this engine (commonly pronounced 'injun') in draining excess water to the notice of the cultivators of *kolpadams* in Mookkuthala. He was present to supervise all aspects of the work, even that of transporting the bamboos.

The fuel required to run the machinery was brought in large barrels which were placed on the platform along with the engine. A thatched hut was built above them which also served as living quarters for the workers. The construction started at the end of Thulaam and was completed in three months. During this period, the engine worked continuously till the waters went down to ankle level. Then the field was ready for cultivation.

We gradually got used to the thunderous sound of the machine working round the clock, every year for three months from Thulaam. But we
children were fascinated by the engine and would often demand to be
taken to see it. In sheer desperation the *irikkanamma*s would have the
servants take out the boats and pile all the children into it to go to the kolpadam. Then they would lift us onto the platform and, though the loud
sound of the engine and the reverberation of the platform were unpleasant, we would watch it, for an hour or two. The sight of the water gushing
out with a roar—'hoong'—through a large pipe filled us with amazement.
Philippose would not be present, only his workers. We saw him when he
came to collect his dues and waited near the illam's front veranda in a
respectful posture. His moustache and the checked *lungi* that he wore
were a source of fascination to us children.

My childhood was closely associated with boats, water tanks, and baths
within the illam and boats and backwaters outside it. But there was an
incident in the month of Karkidagam, in my thirteenth year, when the
sight of water terrified all of us. The day had seemed to be like any other
in the rainy season. But, when we went to bed after dinner, we heard
the portentous sounds of a blustering stormy wind. As it approached, it
developed into a whirlwind and blew branches and leaves from distant
trees onto the four verandas. These soon began to fill the *nadumittam*
and were also forced into the rooms through the bars of the windows.
We could hear the sound of trees swaying in the storm before the wind
uprooted them. We shut all the doors and windows and ran helter-skelter
between the *thekkini* and *vadakkini*. But there was no safety anywhere.
Fear made sleep impossible. By then it had started to rain and together
with the wind it kicked up a storm which the trees near the illam could
not withstand. The sound of the raging tearing trees as they collapsed
penetrated at regular intervals. Fortunately, none of them fell on our
roof.

By dawn, the force with which the wind blew decreased perceptibly.
Its whistling became less shrill. We mustered up the courage to sleep but,
when we woke, there was heavy rain outside. The *antharjanams* could
not go out for a bath. The grounds were filled with leaves and branches
and swirling waters which rose even as we watched and surged into the
northern part of the compound. The well and tanks became one with
the compound. We did not bathe on that day, nor were the usual rituals

of prayer possible. It continued to rain heavily and, though there was water everywhere, we did not realize then that these were indeed flood waters. The rains lasted three days and then, gradually, the waters began to recede.

This happened in 1942. When you compare the dates, M.T. Vasudevan Nair's references to a flood in *Nalukettu* must have been to this one. Many people in the region benefited because they were able to buy logs of wood at low rates. These logs had been borne along by strong currents in the river and people with great daring drew them ashore with stout ropes and sold them to others. In 1943 when I came to Nilayamgode as a bride, I saw that expensive logs of wood, sawed and cleaned, were piled high on the long veranda running round the southern part of the house, the *thekkupuram*.

That time when the waters rose to their doorstep, the mothers in the family were discussing another flood altogether—an earlier one. This was the floods of '99, the Malayalam equivalent of the English calendar 1923–4, four or five years before I was born, a year or two after the Khilafat Movement. Khilafat had struck terror in the Namboodiris in the Mookkuthala region. Soon after, the floods provided yet another reason for panic. Our mothers were discussing the problems that a relation of ours who lived on the banks of the Bharathapuzha had to face. It all started one evening before darkness set in. There was heavy rain and the waters started to creep in. It was thought at first that this was just an overflow of the water filling the compound. But the waters began to surge forward and did not stop rising. When it reached the doorstep, children rejoiced that they could now have a bath right there. But, even as they looked on, the waters entered the house. That was when the older members' stomachs contracted with fear. Theirs was a family where *yagam* was performed and the *yagagni*—the sacrificial fire—had to be protected at all costs. There were three pits with sacrificial fires burning in them in the vadakkini. If these were put out, various rituals including the lighting of fire by friction of the wood of the arani tree to re-invoke the Agnidevata would have to be performed. The Namboodiris therefore placed the fires in three *uris*, and these containers hanging from the ceiling were pulled up as the flood levels mounted.

But the waters rose even higher and lapped against the walls of the rooms. The doors were all left wide open. It was believed that doors had to be shut when the wind blew and left open when water entered the building. The waters pushed with greater force and urgency through the corridors. Everybody went upstairs carrying the vessels. The waters, too, began to creep up the stairs. The sacrificial fire pits had long since been washed away, but now everyone was anxious only for their lives. They spent all night upstairs till the villagers came in the morning to rescue them in their boats.

12 Waiting to Grow Up

Bamboo groves, considered to be essential symbols of the prosperity of a family, pushed up tender shoots once a year, and made music where they stood beside fences at the far end of the grounds. Grandmothers would tell their children waiting eagerly for the advent of Onam that if they sat on the tender bamboo shoots and looked eastward, they would see Onam approaching. Since the bamboos sprouted only once a year, they were called '*aandamula*'—annual bamboo—and they signalled the arrival of Onam. Grandmothers encouraged children to believe that Mahabali came down on earth, stepping on an oval-shaped plank placed at the pointed end of the tender sprouts.

Onam brought with it the riches of flowers, fruits, and vegetables. Flowers bloomed in clusters on fences, hillsides, and fields. Grains and vegetables were in plentiful supply. They were, in literal terms, the first fruits of the labour since Vishu. Nature was worshipped and placated before sowing the seeds after the festival. While the summer vegetables flourished in the fields at Vishu, Onam vegetables were grown in the compound itself. The soil, cool after the summer rains, received the seeds of pumpkins, gourds, long beans, okra, brinjals, green chillies, and ginger and were tended carefully with adequate manure and water. The yellow

* Translated by Indira Menon

creepers were trained onto the low ceilings of the cowsheds, on mud walls, and gate houses. They bore beautiful flowers and laden with vegetables presented a pretty sight.

Pumpkins and long beans grew in greater profusion than other vegetables. Plucking the long beans was interesting work involving many people. The plants grew thickly together and had to be pushed aside to make way for the pickers who tucked up their *dhotis* and used it as a receptacle to gather them. They were then brought to the veranda and piled in a heap. Everyone pitched in to categorize them severally as the dried ones, the seasoned ones, the raw green, and the very tender ones for use variously as seeds, for frying, for cooking with vegetables. The children also joined in enthusiastically. The dry vegetable made of these was thought to be so tasty that a couplet was dedicated to it which said that while many may be required to ready it, I'd insist on being the only one to eat it.

When vegetables were in plenty it was usual to distribute them among relatives and neighbours. Pumpkins which grew in large numbers were placed on round hanging shelves made of strong rope. One pumpkin was put on the lowest rung, a second one on a higher level, and five or six such shelves containing pumpkins placed above them where they stayed fresh for a long time.

The banana trees had been planted the previous year timed to bear fruit at Onam. In those days *nenthrakkaya*—a large variety of the fruit—was a speciality available only at Onam time. The vegetable, yam, which was a necessity at Onam feasts, was dug up even if it was not fully grown.

The paddy, which was sown on an auspicious day after Vishu, would be ready for harvesting at Onam time. After the rains, when the sun put in an appearance, the golden coloured paddy would be reaped, measured, and piled up in the courtyard and the inner halls. The farm workers and other labourers would be doled out generous portions of the grain.

Karkidakam was considered to be a cruel month. But even at that time of distress, there were signs of the approaching prosperity of Onam. Besides, the relentlessness was mitigated by compensations for women. This was the time for their beauty treatment, as well as the prescribed period to address their health concerns.

The beauty routine started with the morning bath when a mixture of fresh turmeric and castor seeds, mashed into powder on the steps of the tank, was smeared on the face. After the bath, *kanmashi*, kohl, was applied to the eyes and sandal paste in the shape of a thick line to the forehead. *Dashapushpam*, ten varieties of medicinal leaves—*karuka, choola, poovankurunnila, krishnakranthi, mookkutti, moshami, nilappana, kayyonni, uzhinja, thiruthali*—were woven together and worn in the hair, imbuing the hair with fragrance and spreading it till late afternoon pleasing even the minds of the wearers. The old saying, 'eat ten leaves and wear ten leaves' acquired fresh significance. Ten varieties of green leaves other than that of the drumstick that were consumed to aid and regulate digestion included—*thalu, thakara, thazhuthama,* leaves of pumpkins, long beans, yam, colocasia, and varieties of spinach. When the raw paddy was pounded, the light red chaff that separated from it was made into a thick paste with jaggery and salt, spread evenly on banana leaves, and roasted over coals. This was called *kanakappam* and it was a mandatory snack every day during the month of Karkkidakam. This red chaff full of vitamins was appropriately called 'gold dust'. Henna was applied to the hands and feet twice a week to protect them from the dampness of the floor during nonstop rains and the regular contact of the hands with water which made them vulnerable to rapidly multiplying bacteria. On the sixteenth day of Karkkidakam, the pungent root of the medicinal plant *koduveli* was dug up from the soil, washed and ground into a paste, an equal quantity of ghee added and consumed to cleanse the system of all poisonous ingestions. In any case by Onam time, women glowed with renewed beauty and better health.

The children waiting for the advent of Onam with bated breath were captivated by the *poovatti* or flower basket specially made for them by the women in carpenters' households. The long, smooth leaves of the *kaitha* were woven together in the shape of a small square receptacle dangling from a long tendril which was used as a handle to hang the basket around the neck when we stepped out from Atham day to gather flowers. Everyone in the family, the guests who arrived, the children of the *irikkanamma* were given one of these. Even after Onam had come and gone, we preserved these baskets for a while.

We did not make elaborate flower arrangements but were content with worshipping a figure of Thrikkakarappan placed in the *nadumittam*. The central figure of Mahabali with Thrikkakarappan on either side was made of rice powder. Even when we rolled the figures into shape, we pierced them with a thin stick extracted from the coconut leaf and stuck *thulasi* spikes, flowers with their stems like *alari, chembaruthi, kolambi* inside them. Pumpkin flowers were secured on thin coconut sticks and used to adorn the figures. The *thumba* flowers we had gathered from fields and the grounds were heaped before the figures. While our friends, the children of the irikkanammas, made colourful flower arrangements in their homes, we had to be content with our customary rituals. These friends helped us to gather thumba flowers, and Amma gifted them *onapudava* every year.

Yet another memory is of the pleasant smell that filled the large hall adjoining the pantry. A variety of new clothes was stored there within a couple of days of Atham. These bundles were meant for the family members and for distributing to others. The special sets of matching clothes meant for the *antharjanams* and their girls were delivered by the cloth merchant Veeramani Swami in his bullock cart. There was enough here for a year's supply to the antharjanams, the helpers, and guests. The handloom dhotis and towels for the Namboodiris arrived directly from the loom while the mill cloth for the managers and others came from Palghat. On the day of Pooradam star, the managers untied the bundles and sorted out the clothes for distribution. The hall echoed with the sound 'kray, kray' of the material being torn into the required lengths. We children walked in and out of the room to inhale the smells of the open bundles of new clothes.

Other than the coloured borders, it was a space filled with the hues of new unwashed cloth and the purity of white material. Colours, vivid or otherwise, were not usually worn.

The distribution of the clothes began on the Uthradam star day. According to the prevailing village customs, workers who practised various trades brought gifts which were handmade by them. These included wooden bowls with handles and wooden ladles, a bow for each of the boys, small knives with handles made of bulls' horns, pretty little metal bowls, and a silver ring for each of the girls. The family, in turn, gave them new clothes. Tenancy contracts even stipulated the offering of ten bunches of large bananas at Onam time. The ones who brought the bananas returned with new clothes. This give and take created a great deal of good will in both and a sense of security in the tenants.

Girls were not given new clothes at Onam till they were nine years old. We longed to grow up faster, waiting to be acknowledged as women and given our rights. Adult women received twelve set *mundus*, four towels, and one gold-bordered *pudava*. These were counted and laid in separate bundles in the *thekkini* from where the women of the family and those who worked for them picked up their share. There was no differentiation. It is interesting to note that the very use of the word—onapudava— encompassed all gifts, whether of clothes or money.

We used to sing a song which described the various kinds of mundus available:

Onam's fast approaching, and
I fancy a special onakkodi.
Achan'll gift me an onappuda,
One with a notable namakkara.
Ammavan 'll gift me a thing of beauty,
An aruthuketty, nothing less.
Ettan'll gift me with great reverence
A radiant, ravishing ratnavali.
Muthachan'll gift me a moothukara,
Early, even on Moolam day,
My beloved'll gift me privately,
An elegant, radiant kasavukara.

There were many waiting for Onam with dreams in their eyes and their hearts eagerly anticipating the flavours of the feasts serving their favourite foods and the sounds and excitement of Kaikottikali.

13 *Thuppettan*

Parvathy Valiyamma was Achan's first wife. I remember five of her children. A few of them had died earlier. Thuppettan was the youngest of the surviving five. Some of the most terrifying memories of my childhood revolve around the poison-cure treatment that used to take place in the manager's portico with Thuppettan as the star performer in them. He had earned great fame as an expert in toxicology by then. His real name was Subramanian. After learning the Vedas, he continued his studies at Pakaravoor gurukulam and became a Sanskrit scholar. He never married.

Thuppettan studied toxicology for a long time under Cheralapram (Cheralappurathu Krishnan Namboodiri) who stayed at our illam to train him. I remember Cheralapram at fifty. Later when he became the guru of the sixth *thampuran* Poomulli Neelakantan Namboodiripad, Cheralapram shifted from Pakaravoor Illam to the aristocrat's house, Poomulli.

Cheralpram was tall and thin and very knowledgeable in his subject. He was from an illam in Peringode near Poomulli and had his sambandham at a Warrier home in the neighbourhood. Achan, having heard of his expertise in treating snakebites, invited him to our illam. After moving to Pakaravoor, his visits to the Warrier house at Peringode dwindled. So

---

* Translated by Radhika P. Menon

whenever his children wanted to see him, their mother brought them to Mookkuthala. They would spend the entire day with us, retiring to the madhom only at night. The lady used to tell us many stories and we always looked forward to her visits.

Thuppettan studied toxicology for five or six years. Victims of snake poisoning were often brought to the illam. At first, they came seeking Cheralapram's treatment. When we lay down to sleep, if we heard the sound of a *manchal*, we knew that someone was being brought over in a carriage for the cure. And our mothers would confirm, 'Yes ... another victim'. The patient as he lay on the manager's portico looked dead. And as soon as we woke up in the morning, we sped to the portico to have a look at him by which time the procedures and treatment would have begun. Two Nair retainers trained in toxicology stayed at the illam to assist Cheralapram who, as the guru, decided the mode of treatment and instructed them. Thuppettan watched the whole procedure and learnt from it. Such was the manner of training in those times.

The medicines required for the treatment were stored at the illam and were readily available at all times. The Nair retainers were instructed to chew certain raw leaves as well as roots and blow very hard on the victim's head. They took turns to do it—as soon as one man straightened up after blowing on the victim's head, the other bent low to repeat the act—and they continued to administer the medicine in this manner without a break. After some time, they continued the process but switched to blowing into the patient's ears. The sounds were so loud that we could hear them even at the spot we stood, a fair distance away. The whole procedure was meant to clear the poison from the head. Its duration was decided by assessing the toxicity of the venom and sometimes extended to several hours. After a long time, the patient would open his eyes. This happened to most patients who were brought to the illam. The exceptions were few. As soon as the patient opened his eyes, a few pepper seeds were placed in his mouth. He was then asked to chew them and describe the taste. The type of the snake that had bitten him was identified on the basis of the taste he described and a treatment, specifically for the cure of *that* snake venom, was then begun.

All the required medicines were prepared at the illam. Most often, the patient would be fit enough to walk home after the second day's treatment. Some, however, stayed on for three days. Only rarely did we see a patient failing to respond to the treatment. If Cheralapram felt certain about failure, he asked the relatives to take the patient back. No victim or patient was allowed to die in the illam.

As soon as the patient could walk, he was taken to the madhom close by. The building was called '*Thottangadi*'. The follow-up treatment with tablets was administered there. Thuppettan was in charge of it. After confirming that the effect of the poison was waning, a treatment called *aayirakudamaaduga* was initiated at dusk. A thousand pots of water were poured over the patient to cool his head. The patient was seated by the side of the well close to the madhom. The well water was first transferred into copper pots and then poured continuously on his head. This treatment ceased only when the patient began to shiver. Although, technically speaking, the term *aayirakudam* meant the use of a thousand pots of water, invariably the patient was cured long before that. He was rubbed down thoroughly, dressed in dry clothes, and taken inside to lie down. He was then served hot, unsalted gruel and permitted to return home the next day.

No payment was accepted from the patients either for the treatment or even for the medicines. Everything was done free of charge, as a kind of charity. Nor were they charged for their food or stay at the madhom. As they left the illam, the patient and accompanying relatives were often speechless with emotion. They could hardly express their gratitude for the new lease of life. Two or three days later, the relatives usually came to the illam with baskets of *aval*, bananas, jaggery, puffed rice and so on. As a result, the larders of the illam were never empty.

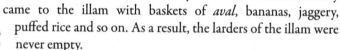

Amidst these usual treatments for snakebites, there was one that filled all the children at Pakaravoor and me, especially, with great dread and anxiety. I must have been five years old then. Nangayya, the daughter of my Valiyamma's eldest son Narayanan Somayajippad, was of my age and we were very close friends. One morning, as we were playing in the courtyard, there suddenly appeared a rabid dog. In sheer fright, I jumped into the arms of an irikkanamma. But the dog charged towards Nangayya, bit her on the thigh and ran away with a chunk of flesh between its teeth. Everyone stood petrified, not knowing how to respond. There was no doctor or hospital nearby. A man was sent to call Cheralapram at once. Cheralapram came to Pakaravoor immediately and bandaged the wound with some medicinal herbs. Nangayya spent the next couple of days in great pain. And then, Cheralapram embarked on an experimental treatment to cure her. If left untreated, the child was sure to die and so Cheralapram readied himself for the gamble.

Four days passed. Nangayya was given a bath early in the morning and placed on an aavanapalaka, a low stool, in the thekke ara, the southern room. Lamps were lit all around. Nangayya was made to take fistfuls of money and place them as offering before deities like Mukkola Bhagavati, Dakshinamoorthy, Guruvayoorappan, and other family gods. By then, all the Namboodiris of the illam had reached the room. Antharjanams were not permitted entry but, as children, we could see it at close quarters. After the puja, Cheralapram began his treatment. I don't know what medicinal herbs he used. He rolled them into a small ball the size of a lemon, placed it on Nangayya's palm, and asked her to eat it little by little. She was on an empty stomach. As soon as she finished taking the medicine, Cheralapram told her to start counting. She started at one, counted up to twenty without mistakes, but soon it started going wrong. Her facial expression altered horribly and her eyes began to roll. Immediately two men, holding her by her arms and legs, took her to a room on top of the bath house and left her there. The doors were then closed and locked. The room had a tiny opening and we tried to peek through it to find out what was happening. After some time, there was a great change in Nangayya. She began to behave like a dog. A thick liquid began to drool from her mouth and she started pawing the walls and the floor. This must have gone on till evening. No one went into that room. By dusk, Nangayya lay on the floor, completely drained. Two or three men opened the door. They took her to the spot by the side of the well for the *aayirakudamaaduga* treatment. After that, she was wiped dry, taken to the same room which had meanwhile been cleaned thoroughly, and made to lie on a mat covered with a cloth. All night long, Namboodiris took turns and stood guard by her. The mothers assembled in the naalukettu and spent the entire time in sleepless anxiety.

Amma lit the traditional lamp and prayed through the night. Nangayya's mother, however, did not fathom the seriousness of her daughter's condition. At dawn, the Namboodiris came to the thekke ara, the southern room, and clanged the chain on the door. The mothers were afraid of opening it. Who knew what news awaited them?

'The child has opened her eyes. We need some hot gruel.'

Nangayya spent four more days in the same room.

Thuppettan became famous as a toxicologist in due course of time and continued to treat patients at the Thottangadi till the end of his days. Many lives were saved in that building.

On the eve of my wedding, Amma sent a maidservant to Thottangadi madhom with the message, 'The girl wishes to see Thuppan. Please come to the illam'. Maybe because he felt I was being married off into a family that had fashionable ways, Thuppettan did not oblige. Many years later, just before his death, Thuppettan expressed a desire to see all of us despite the fact that we dressed in a manner not suited to antharjanams. When we went to see him, he called me to his side and apologized for not coming to see me on the day before my wedding.

Thuppettan's medical dispensary Thottangadi madhom was later demolished. The pathayappura in which he lived stands intact even today, occupied by Jayan, the son of Parameswarettan. But abandoned somewhere in the courtyard, lies the ancient, uniquely-shaped grinding stone that was once used to powder medicines for poison-cures.

14 Attachment

I was five or six years old when two antharjanams, only slightly past their prime, and two young girls, all shabbily dressed, arrived at the back entrance at Pakaravoor carrying a small bundle of clothes. Their faces were swollen with long hours of weeping. Nobody said anything or asked them questions. Yet, everybody understood. One more illam had been attached by court order. Its occupants had no place to go and had, therefore, come here. Amma asked them to have a bath, change their clothes, and eat lunch. After that, they stayed on with us for many years and became a part of Pakaravoor's daily living.

The confiscation of illams was a regular feature of those times. I remember hearing that two illams were attached in Mookkuthala. Even the children who were told these tales by passers-by and those who came to pray at Mookkuthala temple, were filled with fear.

The proceedings were initiated by a clerk of the court sticking a notice on the front door. But even before this, we'd have got news about the attachment from neighbouring illams. I've heard Amma say that earlier, before court papers came into common use, they'd hang strips of palm leaves as notice which, everyone knew, signalled impending distraint. A recent memoir written by a Namboodiri, a renowned artist, spoke of

* Translated by Indira Menon

two illams confiscated because they owed money to Payyappilli Vappu. A member of one of these families was the chess champion Viswanathan Anand's early coach Narayanan, who died recently.

Incurring debts and the consequent attachment of houses were regular occurrences in those days. The head of the household borrowed money mainly to pay his daughters' dowries, which were to the tune of two to three thousand rupees. Families tried to arrange exchange marriages to reduce the payment. But sometimes it became necessary to give cash. In Pakaravoor, the going rate was four thousand. For my wedding, it rose for the first time to ten thousand. It seems that when a girl child was born my father would bundle four thousand rupees in a piece of cloth and put it aside. I have seen the thick cloth bags used for the purpose.

But this was a luxury only a few homes could afford. In most Namboodiri illams, there was just enough to survive on, with rice coming from their leased fields and the jackfruit and mango trees in their compounds yielding six months' supply of vegetables. Beyond this, money was a rarity. Two thousand and three thousand rupees were amounts beyond their imagination. To raise money, they had either to sell or mortgage their leased-out land. Since most families did not have cultivable fields at their doorstep, they had to sell or mortgage the lands tilled by their tenants.

Payyapalli Vappu was one of those who accepted the mortgage and paid the Namboodiris the required amount. Vappu was a rich man who lived near the Naranipuzha boat jetty and owned the only car in the vicinity. In my childhood, I had not seen anyone driving on the dirt tracks of Mookkuthala and so I have a distinct memory of the fair skinned, fat man leaning back against the rear seat of his car.

The householder, unable to redeem his mortgaged land, had to permanently forfeit the fields where the rice for his meals was harvested. When rice was in short supply, the first to be affected was the world of the old women, their daughters, and girl-children. Even without their being aware of the circumstances, they would one day, suddenly, have no rice to eat. It would not affect the Namboodiris to the same extent. They could eat in the oottuppura attached to the temple and earn money performing pujas. They could, without much trouble, be dependants in aristocratic homes and spend their time eating and resting and cracking jokes. When this happened, they rarely returned to their illams and were largely indifferent to the conditions there.

Whom did the women have? When they starved, they were sometimes helped by the Nair women who served them. These women would work in other homes, pounding and threshing rice and crushing it to make beaten rice. Or they would help in cleaning up the compound and the areas surrounding these houses. They would share some of the rice they were given as payment with their Namboodiri mistress and also supply them with vegetables growing in the compound.

The need for money and the pangs of hunger would force the householder to mortgage other things. The next to go would be his wife's gold *thaali* chain. This was a gold chain stringing together several small oval-shaped thaalis given by the family after her wedding, which she wore till she became a widow. Until then, it was hers. When that was mortgaged, all that remained would be a small single gold thaali strung on a thread and fastened round her neck as a symbol of marriage. First the tenanted land, then the gold chain, then the compound surrounding the illam—one by one they were all mortgaged. The senior Namboodiri would send for Vappu and the money would reach the illam.

When the compound was no longer theirs, the atmosphere inside the illam would undergo a change. The eldest Namboodiri would sit on the veranda with nothing much to do. The younger brothers and other men would move around aimlessly in various parts of the illam. Vappu's workers would come to cultivate the land around the house, now theirs. They would dig the soil, plant saplings, mend the fences. They were within their rights to do so. Their work would also require them to go to the backyard used by the women. This was not out of any evil intention. But then, the women and girls sitting inside, wearing only twin pleated mundus, found it impossible to go even to the kitchen tank nearby. They would have to finish their bath early and take refuge inside before the workers arrived. The glances coming their way through the bars of the window filled them with a new fear, a sense of insecurity. This fear, like a heavy silence, permeated every nook of the house.

The householder would be forced to borrow more. All that remained was the house in which they lived. Then one day, the court clerk would stick the notice on their door and, with that, they would leave, one by one,

silent and without anything tangible to fall back on. The women wearing
dirty clothes and the single thaali still around their necks, would move out
carrying a small bundle of clothes, while the little girls would be in tears at
something they could not comprehend.

The four people who came to Pakaravoor that evening were the victims
of this confiscation. Both mothers stayed there for a while. Then, leaving
their girls behind to cook for us, they went away to some other illam.

In such cases, the grandmothers would usually be sent to their family
homes. The mothers would go to theirs if the families had enough food
to feed them. The young girls would be sent elsewhere to work for their
living. Sometimes, even before the confiscation proceedings began, the
women would start moving out. The master of the house himself would
sometimes send the women to various places and then go his own way.
They were quite indifferent to how their wives and children fared.

The two girls who came that evening stayed with us in Pakaravoor for
eight long years and were treated like family members. Nobody saw them
as outsiders. Their younger brother found work somewhere, made money,
and repossessed their house. He took his sisters away and soon after, got
them married.

During their stay in Pakaravoor, not once did I hear of their father's
visits, though he was working as a priest in a temple not far away. I don't
know whether he married again but he probably continued to crack jokes
and make witty remarks whenever he found an audience.

15 Widows

M.R.B. married Uma Antharjanam, the widowed sister of V.T. Bhattathiripad's wife Sridevi Antharjanam, on 13 September 1934. This historically significant event unsettled and agitated the orthodox Namboodiris and aroused turbulence in the community. I was six or seven years old at the time and I saw the couple only eight or nine years later at a meeting of a social welfare organization in Shukapuram. I had heard that Uma Antharjanam had agreed to remarry after much discussion and coaxing but, by the time I saw her at the meeting, she was already transformed into an enthusiastic, self-confident woman.

M.R.B. was not the only person to marry a widow. His brother Premji, a well-known poet and actor, made a similar daring move in marrying Paryarath Kuriyedath Arya Antharjanam, a young widow. Premji and his wife had accompanied the M.R.B. couple to the meeting at Shukapuram.

I worked in a minor capacity in the social welfare organization and its women's wing till the end of the 1940s without coming across a single other instance of widow remarriage. One reason could be that marriages to old men had almost ceased as a result of the activities of this organization. Also, the younger sons of the Namboodiri families had started marrying

* Translated by Indira Menon

women from their own community. Therefore, the number of widows had also declined. Altogether, the widow's plight in the family had shown comparative improvement.

But earlier in the 1920s and 1930s when I was a child, the situation was different. The condition of the widows in my own home, Pakaravoor, was harsh and pitiful. My father's uncle Pullanapalli, though past seventy, had re-married twice in order to finance the weddings of his two daughters by his first wife. He had no children by his later wives. Though he died soon after, one of his wives lived for a long time in Pakaravoor, doing chores like helping to feed the children, dressing them, and combing their hair. We already had three or four widowed antharjanams employed to work in the kitchen. They took care not to participate in any auspicious ceremony or even to be seen by others, and made sure that they conformed to all the observances prescribed for widows.

In the Namboodiri community, nothing was considered a greater sign of misfortune than the sight of a widow. She was unwanted and referred to as the woman without the marital symbol, the thaali around the neck. It was a bad omen to see her on any auspicious occasion. In those days, many young girls had lost their husbands even before they had emerged from childhood. Paapti Valiamma of the Nilayamgode family into which I married had been brought there as a bride when she was nine years old. She was widowed at sixteen. Her friend Savitri was ten and her husband thirteen when they were married and their life together, lasting two years, had passed like a child's game of fun and games. Her playmate died of typhoid fever, for which there was no known cure, but she continued to live with the family for sixty-five years doing household chores.

After the marriage ceremony, the Namboodiri bride was formally received in her marital home. Usually, this rite followed soon after the wedding but sometimes there was an interval between the two. I know of a girl who was to go to her husband's house a month after the wedding. Before this could happen, the husband died. A girl had no place in her parents' home after marriage. She could not be taken to her husband's either. What was to be done? The priests were in a dilemma. Their solution was that the girl should go to her husband's house accompanied by two or three antharjanams who, at the inauspicious hour of twilight, must kick open the kitchen door, take the girl inside, and leave. Nobody welcomed her with a lighted lamp. All her life was spent in this darkness.

It was believed that the husband's death was caused by the ill-fated alignment of stars in his wife's horoscope. So the widow was held guilty of a criminal act from the moment of his death.

Soon after the demise, the first rite is for the son or stepson to prostrate himself before her and ask her to remove the thaali, the symbol of her married status. She does so without cursing him only because he is her son. Before the cremation, she throws herself at her husband's feet, as if asking forgiveness for her culpability. The pyre is then lit. Afterwards, she has a bath but is not allowed to dry herself or change out of her wet clothes. She can wipe her head and body with the tip of her wet mundu. Even during the heavy rains of Karkidakam, she remains wet and dripping inside a darkened room with the windows shut. She stays there for ten days till the end of the *pula*, the period of defilement, without changing her clothes or seeing anybody. She eats only once a day during this period—uncooked food, unsalted, such as raw bananas and root vegetables roasted over live coal, in addition to ripe bananas and water. She takes a dip in the pond three times a day and back in her room, lies down on the bare floor. But in my childhood, widows were allowed to sleep on a mat made of palm leaves. In the vadakke ara of the nalukettu, two or three women spent those days wet, hungry and weak, cursing themselves. The only relief in sight was the end of the squabbles with their co-wives.

After the ten days considered to be impure, they, together with their children, observed a year of deeksha, after which they could visit temples. But they could not participate in any auspicious functions during that year. They attended weddings, eager to eat good food, but they could not be present at the bride's kudiveppu. I have witnessed the abuses and the humiliation heaped on a widow who was accidentally pushed off a crowded veranda to the space where the ceremony was being performed. After she was married, a girl had to live in her husband's house. Though completely isolated after his death, she was very seldom allowed to go to her parents' house. Even if her mother or father or brother was alive, a woman who was given away would not get much sympathy from them. They disassociated themselves by blaming her fate. Perhaps it was the horrifying state the widows lived in that prompted all the women's prayers, pujas, and fasts for the longevity of their husbands. Retaining her married state was considered to be a woman's greatest good fortune. Therefore, leisure time was mostly devoted to holding the thaali and reciting mantras for the husband's well being. In the Tamil Brahmin community, the widows' state did not seem to have been so bad though it was a pitiful sight to see their hair being cut and their heads shaved. The unfortunate shaven Brahmin women were not considered an auspicious sight. But they were not shut up in the house because they did not have to observe the isolation practised by the antharjanam. Fasts may also have been fewer. Widowhood brought about changes in the dress as well. They were not to smear *chandanam*, sandalwood paste, on their forehead. Instead, they could apply only moistened *bhasmam* or the holy ash. The only piece of jewellery they were allowed was the ring worn at the time of their husbands' funeral rites, the *pavitramothiram*, which they could continue to wear afterwards. As for their clothes, the antharjanams did not generally wear any festive clothes, so the difference was merely in the width of the border—the neem leaf design for married women and the stylus design for widows. The border was narrow. The married women wore, in addition, a gold bordered mundu and had a long mull cloth to wrap around them when they went out, but the widows were denied these. The cloth merchant Veeramani Swami from Pattambi delivered to Pakaravoor quantities of both types of material, loaded on to a bullock cart. I still remember the annual arrival of this cart. Veeramani's shop in Pattambi has prospered since then.

Achan died when I was two years old and in my memory, Amma was always a widow. She observed all the fasts and rites strictly, fasting all day on 'Ekadashi', the eleventh day from the full moon or the new moon. I remember her feeling weak and tired during Shravanam when she fasted on both 'Ekadashi' and 'Dwadashi', the eleventh and twelfth days, without even a sip of water. In spite of this, on 'Thrayodashi', the thirteenth day, she would drink water only after the ritual of a bath, a visit to the temple, and the performing of Vishnu puja. Her throat must have been parched after long periods of continuous fasting. But, compared to the plight of other widows, Amma's situation was not so pitiable. This must have been because of the respect and consideration that she continued to receive from the family and society. Amma earned this through her personality. Among those who were widowed early were some intelligent, good-looking, brave women who learned Sanskrit and conducted the Bhagavatha Saptaham, the seven-day religious discourse of the Bhagavatham, in an attempt to get on with their lives. I am reminded of Karoor's story, 'Poovambhazham', about a beautiful antharjanam whose emotions came to nothing. It describes how widows watch young Namboodiris through the bars of the vadakkini window as they eat their meals or move about in the *thekkini*. Though widow remarriage was advocated by V.T. and others as part of the reforms, no widow came forward to accept the offer. V.T.'s sister-in-law Uma, a widow, finally gathered courage to remarry after a great deal of counselling. M.R.B. married Uma in Rasika Sadanam in the presence of several national leaders, associates in V.T.'s crusade. The well-known social worker Arya Pallom enthusiastically participated in the happy occasion even though her son had died just three days before. I was only six or seven years old at the time. Our servants and passers-by spoke of it as a calamity and added their curses. The antharjanams labelled it as self-willed wantonness. I heard them say 'Why didn't that accursed widow spend her remaining years praying instead of setting out on this course?'

The Namboodiri society excommunicated M.R.B. and Premji, barring them from entering Namboodiri houses or temples. When I arrived in Nilayamgode as a bride, I learned that M.R.B. and V.T. with their wives, were regular guests there. Though they were forbidden to take a bath in ponds belonging to illams, this edict was disregarded in Nilayamgode. The antharjanams who visited Nilayamgode were undecided about whether or not to meet them. They satisfied their curiosity by looking at these married women without the customary thread round their necks, from a distance. Orthodoxy takes time to be rooted out. Premji's younger son Induchoodan later married Mani, my second elder brother's daughter. When that wedding was arranged, the bride's grandmother is said to have asked, 'You have only one daughter. Why must you give her to the son of a remarried-widow?' That was twenty-eight years ago. That grandmother is no longer alive. If she were, she, too, may have changed.

16 I Know Lucy

Lucy, a character in Srimathi Sarah Joseph's novel, *Mattathi*, touched me deeply. Lucy has no memory of a mother who had discarded her at birth or of a father whom she had never seen. She lives with an aunt doing endless chores under her supervision. She glimpses the sky between the branches of a *moringa* tree, briefly inhales the fresh air, and convinces herself that she has no other birthright. She caresses the cows, the sheep, and the chickens, chatters to them, and learns the first lessons of love.

Only the laundress Cherona understands her. When, as a special concession, her aunt allows her to join college, Cherona takes out two small bodices from her bundle and gives them to her. 'Wear these when you go to college. Otherwise the boys will not take their eyes off your chest.' Lucy has never seen a bodice before. This is her first introduction to her femininity and its manifestation and it encourages her to look at her body and admire its form. She wants other people to notice her. When she sees the boys in college grab food from the girls' lunch boxes, she longs for them to take her food too. She is attracted to Sethu, her classmate. She likes the scent and proximity of Varghese, the man who cuts down bananas ready for ripening. She wistfully witnesses the overt expressions of love between

* Translated by Indira Menon

Celina and her husband who visited them once. She tries to shut herself in a room and breastfeed Celina's baby.

We see Lucy pining for the acceptance of her femininity and longing for motherhood. I know many such Lucys, have known their yearning, their desires, and fears, at close quarters. They lived, unwanted, in the inner quarters of illams, in their kitchens, as one of the many wives of their husbands. If girls died unmarried, it was believed the family would suffer misfortune. Therefore, parents took desperate measures to get them married. Even if the man was disfigured or diseased, they would not be deterred. The girl may not, then, be forced to go to her husband's house. But what about those who were taken to their marital homes full of expectations about wedded bliss? The father had fulfilled his responsibility but the girls were targeted by angry women, their husband's other wives. Sometimes the husbands did not even touch them but their identities were circumscribed by the thaali chain, by the mere satisfaction of being married. They had nothing of their own, their lives had come to naught, and their marriages were merely concessions made to their existence.

These women would rejoice from a distance when sons were born to their husband's favourite wife. The thought that, even if they were abandoned in life, their spirits would not have to wander unredeemed after death was a cause for celebration. This son born of the common husband would perform the final rites for salvation in their afterlife. On his birthday and at other special functions, they would immerse themselves in prayers at the various temples nearby, gathering flowers as offerings to the deity. 'Dhaara' would be performed at Shiva temples and prayers conducted for the boy's long life and good fortune. Though born of their husband's other wife, he had the power to elevate their wandering spirits to the higher plane inhabited by their departed forefathers. They comforted themselves that this son, through prayers and sacrificial offerings, would raise them to the status of the gods and respected forefathers. Ignoring the seclusion of their lives, they would from afar love and bless the guardian of their afterlives. When the little boy grew older and started to eat his meals in the kitchen, they would peer at him from behind the slits in the door.

Lucy's abandoned state brought these pictures vividly back to mind.

17 Betel Nuts

The cardinal requisite of hospitality in Kerala homes was the offering of a plate of betel leaves and its accompaniments arranged on a burnished brass plate or in an engraved betel box. Both men and women chewed it regularly. Family members expressed satisfaction when guests sat down for a short session of gossip punctuated by betel chewing. On special occasions, the plate was elaborately decorated, a practice that is continued to this day.

When Namboodiris spent their time indulging in idle talk, a plentiful supply of betel leaves and its accompaniments were always ready on hand. 'Lounging on the front veranda, chewing and spitting betel juice, satirizing shiftless people' is how the saying goes. Since many Namboodiris used to come and stay in Pakaravoor, betel leaves were always placed on the front veranda. The plate had to include a special kind of betel nut called *neettadakka*. Arecanut, when fully ripe, was dried in the sun and soaked in clay and earthen jars filled with water. This remained in the water for several months without going bad. The man in charge of the pantry scooped them out, removed the outer fibre, washed and discarded the skin, and readied it for use. A large bell-metal receptacle containing lime, plentiful

* Translated by Indira Menon

first quality tobacco and betel leaves were arranged on the plate contributing to the enjoyment of lounging on the front veranda.

Women chewed betel leaves three times a day as a ritual observed by those belonging to aristocratic families, first after brushing their teeth every morning, later after lunch, and then before going to bed. Therefore, they always had a betel leaf box at hand. They sat around the nadumittam chewed betel leaves and spat the juice into it. It was however forbidden for a woman to chew tobacco. They were expressly permitted to use what was commonly referred to as the 'three ingredients'—tender betel leaves, lime, and *kaliyadakka*—thereby obliquely criticizing those who added tobacco to the three.

It was imperative for women to have kaliyadakka in their betel box. The reddish tinted shiny black kaliyadakka was considered a status symbol of the family. It needed great expertise to achieve the right combination of colour, lustre, and fragrance.

Kaliyadakka was made from arecanut which was neither too ripe nor too green. It was not easy to procure this and they had to regularly pester the man who cut the nuts down from the trees for the ones with the required ripeness, no more nor less.

The skies cleared after four months of continuous rain and welcome sunshine brightened the courtyards. This was the right time to make kaliyadakka.

The nuts were separated from the bunches and were boiled and cooled in their shells. This outer covering was then removed and they were stewed for over a week in a heavy bell metal vessel filled with water placed on a fire which was sometimes kindled and at other times extinguished. The softened nuts were cut into thin round slices and spread out in the sun to dry. The residual water was a thick liquid which was re-heated for a short time daily for a few days till it acquired the consistency of a jelly called 'kali'. When the pieces were dry, a part of the paste in the ratio of 1:3 was again thickened over the fire, and rubbed individually on each piece. This process was repeated once again. Whatever remained of the kali liquid was further gelatinized after adding jaggery to it. When the mixture turned dark brown, spices such as clove, cardamom, caraway seeds, and liquorice were crushed and added to the jelly to coat the nuts. The nuts which were rolled up into a round shape when mixed with the hot brown gel, acquired a lovely hue on cooling and drying. The shining reddish black nuts, redolent with the fragrance of spices, presided regally over the betel plate of the women and became a symbol of their skill and status.

An arecanut grove on the grounds where the family residence stood was considered to augur well for the household because it was a sign that soil was not dry. Arecanut trees needed a great deal of water especially in the summer. Usually banana trees, some laden with fruit and others not, grew thickly in its proximity and, at its edges, as if on guard, stood coconut trees bent with the weight of coconuts. A cluster of colocasia plants with their leaves unfurled served to enhance the loveliness of the grove. Such aesthetically pleasing woodlands which also served to cool the area, conserve water, and create wealth for the owner, merged seamlessly with the traditions of the village. From sunrise to sunset, our daily requirements were closely intertwined with the produce of these trees.

The trees were remarkable because every part of them could be put to daily use. While the coconut tree was honoured with the title of 'kerakalpam' (the rejuvenating coconut), the arecanut tree has equally to be praised for its contribution. Each part of the arecanut tree was used and nothing was discarded. When I look back on my early days, my respect for these trees increases greatly. The only garment we girls wore till we were nine years old was a loincloth made either by tying together two strips of banana leaves heated over a flame to prevent tearing, or a strip of the tender film of the arecanut spathe. We preferred the latter. Our maidservants gathered them from the ground where they lay scattered and got them ready for our use by separating the film and hooking it on a string. When they took us to the pond in the morning, they wet the loincloth in water and softened it for us. Till the evening when we changed it, the loincloth remained supple and lay softly against our skin.

Relatives who came from regions where arecanut trees did not grow in profusion took several of these when they returned. When the floor was smeared with cow dung, the excess was removed with pieces of the ripened spathe called 'palak' which, too, they stuffed into their bundles. The vadakkini where spiritual and religious rites were conducted was cleaned with cow dung by antharjanams themselves. From the age of ten girls were taught not to feel revulsion for dirt by making them handle cow dung. This was a lesson to us that a woman needed to face the battles of life with equanimity and calm.

In my village Mookkuthala, arecanut groves flourished in the wet soil surrounding overflowing back waters. We were always amazed at a different sight when we passed Vanneri, the village next to ours by the seaside. Rows of coconut trees stood laden with heavy bunches of the fruit, thriving even when no special care was lavished on them. The earth's largesse enabled different areas to grow the produce unique to them.

If a thatched shed had to be raised on special occasions, four arecanut trees were cut down to hold up the ten bundles of dry coconut leaves used as the thatch. This allowed for good ventilation and kept the enclosure cool.

Summer was the time for celebrations, when deities emerged from inside the temple walls into the open. When they arrived at each doorstep, devotees welcomed them with a *para* filled with paddy arranged around an arecanut *pookkula* or inflorescence. The bigger its size, the less the paddy needed to fill the para. The green and yellowish seeds on the efflorescence enhanced its beauty. After the welcoming ceremony, the flowerage was divided among the children. But there were also times when it was taken to decorate the neighbour's para and the children were left to cry.

On all auspicious occasions, this cluster of flowers was on display as symbols of prosperity. During temple festivals, the deities were welcomed by young girls carrying decorated platters which also had a stem of the arecanut florescence to add to its splendour. The young girl would hold a bunch of this flowerage, sitting in the *kalam* or the space where figures of deities are drawn with coloured powder such as upon the occasion of the *sarpathullal*. After worshipping the snakes on the day of the Aayilyam star, the grains of the pookkula were mixed with milk and poured over the sacred stone. (However at weddings, the coconut efflorescence had pride of place.)

The farmer sported a headgear made from the spathe of the arecanut as his identity. The poor used it to make handheld fans to counter the summer heat. The fans made from palmyra palm leaves with decorated edges were few in number. Most people used arecanut fans which were readily available. Villagers drew water from the well in a spathe stitched together on both sides. The phrase used—spathe and rope—indicated the manner in which it was done.

After the harvest of *mundakan* paddy, farmers grew a year's supply of vegetables in the field. The creepers of pumpkin, gourd, and cucumber were trained on to the dry bark of the arecanut tree gathered from the grounds. Other vegetables like the bitter gourd, bottle gourd, *koval*, etc., were trained to climb on to the shed with the help of this bark. When the cucumber began to ripen, it was placed in a spathe to prevent it from losing its fresh colour. The white, clean spathe, holding a golden cucumber within it, was considered to be an auspicious sight at Vishukkani.

Those who owned a large arecanut grove found it to be a useful source of fuel. The bark and the spathe of the tree were used to light the fire in the courtyard to boil paddy.

Each year, fully ripened arecanuts were sown in the groves and transplanted at the foot of the old ones in the proportion of two hundred sprouted seeds to an acre of land. Sunlight did not penetrate the groves where arecanut and banana trees grew thickly side by side. Many arecanut trees were lost every year. The new seedlings were planted in spaces left vacant by the trees felled by strong winds or cut down for use. Today, water shortage does not permit such transplanting. It has become difficult even to conserve the existing ones. In the olden days, yoked bullocks were used to draw water from the well to water the grove. In summer months, channels were dug for the water to flow out to the trees.

The plucking season added to the charm of the courtyard smeared and cleaned with cow dung. We could stare endlessly at the gold coloured, red tinged nuts piled up there. As an offering to the deity or to Brahmins on auspicious occasions, a shining whole nut was placed on tender betel leaves before a burning lamp.

Today, villages celebrate temple festivals with great pomp. But in earlier times, rice gruel and curried lentil were served free to large numbers of people in an arecanut spathe pinned together on all sides with small sticks. Today, this is served on spathe plates moulded by machines. These are donated in large numbers by devotees to the temples for such use. The arecanut has an important place in Kerala's economy.

Families which depended on paddy cultivation for their livelihood had to rely on the yield to meet all their needs. They used the grain not only as food but also to pay their workers and to buy essential goods. This included wages to the dhobi, the barber, the midwife. Harvest time was when all debts were repaid. At such difficult times, the income from the arecanut grove came as a great relief. These groves did not require much capital expenditure. Green leaves, wood ash, cow dung, the chaff available after the harvest together with plenty of water in the shallow pits dug around the trees, were sufficient to get a good yield.

The major market for arecanut was Pazhanji. Arecanut trees bloomed in the monsoon and, at the time of plucking by the end of Dhanu, had eight or ten bunches with thirty to fifty nuts in each. As soon as the bunches were cut down, they were taken by boat to Pazhanji to be sent on to various parts of India. This was transformed into fragrant betel nuts by centres in Bangalore and Calcutta. They were also in demand in paint manufacturing units.

The sandy areas near the sea were the golden spaces for coconut cultivation. This coconut belt stretched nearly ten kilometres inland. Arecanuts thrived in a mixture of sand and soil. These wetlands were the arecanut belt. In such ideal soil, the trees were planted only two feet apart from each other to facilitate movement from the top of one tree to the next while cutting the bunches.

Diseases like *mahali* sometimes attacked these trees and the whole family, even the children, were afraid that their source of supplementary income in the coming year would be destroyed. Spraying insecticide and other measures were adopted to overcome the problem. The middlemen who had contracted to buy these nuts were also equally affected by this development.

Today, women are not interested in making kaliyadakka. The antharjanam's betel leaf plate is no longer fragrant with the nuts nor does it hold such colours. Instead they are resplendent with the hues of the fragrant lime and Roja betel nuts. Arecanuts, piled high on the roadside, are now a rare sight when we travel past Pazhanji and Chalisseri.

18 Leavings

Feasts played a major role in my childhood experiences.

Almost every other day there was something big or small to celebrate, not only in Pakaravoor but in all the wealthy homes of the time. The large number of people assembled for a feast was considered to be indicative of the status of the head of the family in the community. The guests were not actually invited. They only needed to hear about the festivity to attend it. Most townspeople knew whose birthday fell on what date and they would flock to the celebration. Invitations were sent out only for weddings and it was the responsibility of the servants and the women companions of the antharjanam to deliver them.

Birthday celebrations were among the most important of these but not all birthdays were given equal significance. The Namboodiris and their sons were feted lavishly but the women and girl-children had to be content with just one extra item added to their daily meal. There were special pujas for the long life of the men and their sons in temples and illams. But not for the women. In Namboodiri homes nobody prayed for their longevity.

Sometimes the feasts were held in temples and, at other times, in the illam. In the first case, the *vaaram* with its Vedic chants followed by an

* Translated by Indira Menon

elaborate meal was conducted as an offering to the deity. Some vaarams were held on a large scale with the one-thousand-banana vaaram leading the rest. This meant that a thousand ripe bananas were peeled, cooked, and made into a jam which was used to make a *prathaman*. God was not interested in this sweet, nor was it offered to the deity. This was only to pander to the greed of those who had arrived to eat to their hearts' content. All the traditional items which were prescribed for it such as *erissery*, *pulissery*, *kaalan*, *olan*, eight different fried items, and eight different pickles in addition to the prathaman, were served. Curries like *rasam* and *sambhar* which were not indigenous and which required asafoetida or onions to be added to them were not included since these were not permitted on the temple premises. Namboodiris and children ate there and food was sent home for the women.

The most lavish of all the feasts was the kudiveppu when the new bride was brought to her husband's home. In those days, the eldest son married more than once but the festivities were held on a grand scale only the first time. There would be feasting for two or three days. Group dances (*panenkali*) and religious rites (*sathram*) were a part of this. The first time I saw this group dance was after my second elder sister's wedding. I was only eight but even at that time it did not interest me. Recently I watched it again on television and dismissed it as a monotonous dance form with no art content whatsoever. I wondered why people celebrated movements which had no divine, artistic, or entertainment value, only vulgarity.

In Pakaravoor, thatched structures were not erected to hold feasts since there were many large halls built for the purpose. These were known as the *kettu* and the largest of them was called the *nataka shala*. Most wealthy homes had a nataka shala for Kathakali dances or religious rites. Though my family was far removed from drama or any art form, the kettu continued to be called nataka shala. During major functions like the kudiveppu or *vaara sadya*, it doubled up as dining space when the temple could not accommodate the large number of guests.

The children were fed first, then the Namboodiris, and finally the women. When the first two sets of people had eaten, the maidservants removed the used leaves and cleaned the floor. But when the last round was over, the used leaves were left in place for food to be served to the Nair women who had accompanied the Namboodiri women as helpers.

These helpers always went with antharjanams, walking ahead of them even on a trip to the nearest temple. One of their duties was to order the lower castes to make way for the antharjanam. Yet another duty was to carry the children; if an antharjanam had two or three, she would be allowed as many helpers. If a person of a lower caste strayed into their path, the woman would draw a line on the ground which the person was asked not to cross. Then she would measure the distance between them and the line to determine whether the antharjanam had been polluted by the untouchable. If the approaching person was a carpenter, then it was important to check whether he was carrying his measuring rule, because if he was, his presence did not sully the antharjanam.

Antharjanams and their companions were not invited to the feasts. Nevertheless, they arrived because they had the right to be present. These women timed their trips to the Guruvayoor and Mookkuthala temples to coincide with birthdays and other festivities because they longed for good food. The family, realizing that feasting was of paramount importance and that not everyone ate well in their homes, always made provision for the large numbers. It was quite common for women and children to invoke the goddess's blessings, praying for enough food to eat at the feast.

The antharjanams, arriving with their helpers, tucked their umbrellas in the gap between the wall and the roof tiles and went in through the rear entrance of the oottuppura. The helpers waited in the bath house near the tank, or in the shack where rice was pounded or sat on the back veranda with the children on their laps, rubbing their own tired feet. They stayed on for at least four or five days.

When the antharjanams had eaten, it was the turn of these helpers waiting hungrily outside to be called for lunch. They would entrust the children to their mistress so as to be ready to go in when they were summoned by the irikkanammas. We children often went there to watch the crush and confusion caused by their rushing forward and crowding near the door.

But these women straining to go in would not be allowed easy entry. A Brahmin cook would stand at the door keeping one half of it shut and physically blocking their way. As she approached the door, each helper had to call out the name of the house she worked for and, if the irikkanamma approved, the cook would move his arm and allow her to enter. No one was admitted without this verification. The rejected ones were fed only after everyone else had eaten.

What awaited them inside were the used and dirty banana leaves on which the half-eaten food of the antharjanams still lay spattered. Some would turn the leaves over so as to have their rice and curry served on the 'clean' side, only to find that the dust from the several feet traversing the floor of dry cow dung paste was stuck to the reverse. Others would push the half-eaten food away to make some fresh space but the *payasam* flowing across the leaf did not always guarantee a clean surface. These women did not have the right or the patience to look for an unused leaf.

Even before the women attempted to clean the dirty leaves, the servers would arrive one after another. The servings were generous, everything was in plenty, and of the same quality as given to the others. The only stipulation was that they had to eat off used banana leaves.

There was no shortage of banana leaves in my house even though more than half the month was taken up by feasts. The room adjoining the *oottuppura* was used to store several bundles of these. When I think of this, I always wish that these poor women were served on at least a torn piece of a clean leaf. They were humiliated in so many ways—in their very life as helpers, in having to rush forward to be granted admittance to the oottuppura, and finally, in being forced to eat on used banana leaves! Why did I not, like Satyavati in *Prathama Prathisruthi*, clamour for Amma's intervention? I wish now that I had had the sense to voice my protest, especially when I remember that one of those dirty leaves, spread out for the women to eat from, was indeed mine.

For antharjanams, too, eating off used leaves was a part of life. After four days of wedding ceremonies, the woman became a wife only when she fed off the leftover leaf used by the husband. The bride served him and, as he ate, poured a little water into his cupped palm. When he got up, she placed her right hand on the leaf and then used the same leaf to eat from. This practice would be continued regularly thereafter.

It was when I had begun to think that these tales of leftover food were no longer relevant that I happened to read the autobiographies of some Dalit writers. Om Prakash Valmiki's story *Echil* (*Joothan* in Hindi) was one of these. The leavings of upper caste people were collected in baskets and dried by the Bhangis for consumption later. In Sharankumar Limbale's story 'Akkarmasi', we see Dalits separating wheat grains from cow dung and using them to cook chapattis. Their food is culled from faeces. In yet another autobiography, the theme is hunger and half eaten leftover food. If my tales belong to another time, these narratives speak of the present. The cruelty and injustice of the past continue to haunt us in many forms, the worst of these being the feeding of leavings. I am almost forced to believe that nothing defines the Indian identity more than half-eaten leftover food.

19 Smallpox

Krishnan, whom everyone called Unni, was Achan's grandson. Achan was also named Krishnan and, since it was forbidden for *Amma* to utter his name, she referred to him as Unni and others did the same. Achan's grandson was of the same age as my own brother, Neelakantan.

Unni was a handsome boy with an attractive smile. He was also very intelligent and active in the welfare organization's mixed feeding programme where Namboodiris mingled with people of other and lower castes. The community ostracized him for this and he left home with my other brothers to join an educational institution run by a Namboodiri in Trichur. He did not seek anyone's permission or even inform others of his decision. He was only fifteen or sixteen years old at the time and had completed his early education.

Four or five years passed. Unni was staying in a lodge with some others near the school in Trichur. One day, he was taken ill with a fever and his lodge-mates brought him to Pakaravoor the same night.

Neither Unni nor his friends knew the nature of the illness. That night he slept with others in the pathayappura where the Namboodiris stayed.

* Translated by Indira Menon

In the morning, the men, including my brothers, appeared to be in a state of panic when they came out. Krishnan, who had spent the night with them, had high fever and pustules had appeared all over his body.

It was a case of smallpox.

It was a time when this disease terrified everyone. Nobody dared name the word, referring to it merely as 'the illness'. There was no known cure and a fourth of those who had contracted it succumbed. Even those who recovered were left disfigured, their faces pitted with deep pox marks. It left some totally blind and others with vision in only one eye, the latter striking greater terror in most of us.

When the Namboodiris discovered the nature of Unni's illness, they panicked, but finally decided to move him to a Brahmin madhom in Thottangadi, a furlong away.

The women and children in the *nalukettu* were not aware that Unni had taken ill and had arrived at night. It was only in the morning that Krishnan *Pattar* and Srinivasan Pattar who came in at the back door to make coffee informed us about this development: 'Krishnan Namboodiri was taken ill and brought in last night .They are moving him to Thottangadi madhom. You can go and see him now if you like.'

It was believed that this illness had no cure. When anyone contracted this dreaded disease the rest of the family left the illam, abandoning the afflicted one. The front doors remained open but the parents, brothers, sisters, grandmothers provided the patient with some drinking water and went away to other known homes, carrying a hastily collected bundle of clothes. No one was turned back at such times.

The people specially assigned to look after the sick ones were those who had earlier recovered from the pox. Every village had a couple of these and they were bound by convention to attend on the infected as a way of thanking God for having saved them. They were, therefore, quite willing to care for the patient when they were sent for. Those who had been severely affected were deemed to be the fittest to nurse the afflicted one. These people were presumed to be totally dedicated to the patient and they would stay on till the end was known one way or the other.

There was an additional problem if the afflicted one was a Namboodiri. The caregivers had necessarily to be other Namboodiris or Brahmins because even water given by people of a lower caste defiled them. Such a situation was considered to be worse than death.

It was not usual for the caregivers to work alone—there were always two of them since the frightening nature of the disease could not be borne without support. Dedication to their duty which was to remove the phlegm from the patient's throat, clean the eyes, feed him drops of rice gruel, and wet the parched lips, was of paramount importance.

The patient's recovery depended a great deal on the skill of the caregiver. The story goes that a certain Namboodiri who had been given up for dead was revived when a new caregiver arrived on the scene and removed the phlegm from his throat, clearing the air passage.

Caregivers were sent for immediately when Unni fell ill. It was decided to move him to the madhom even before they came. Srinivasa Pattar announced to us, 'Unni is being moved. All those who want to see him can do so now'.

We went out through the main doors of the hall used at various times as the dining space and the Kaikottikali arena. The children lined up quietly at the entrance and the women stood just behind the open door. The servants watched from the courtyard. No one spoke; fear was palpable in the air. Unni came down the stairs alone from the pathayappura. He had a *mundu* around his waist and had wrapped another around his body. As he went down the steps of the large hall where the Namboodiris usually assembled, he turned to look at us but we could not read the expression on his face. We watched him go through the southern part of the courtyard, the thekkupuram until he was out of sight. Mothers and grandmothers were too paralysed to even recite their prayers.

Soon the caregivers arrived—two Brahmin men who were directed to the madhom. It was fortunate that they were located immediately; otherwise the patient would have had to lie unattended for two or three days.

Unni lay ill for nine days. Each day, one of the caregivers came up to the entrance and called out the progress report. 'Unni opened his eyes and drank some water'. Again, 'He is a little weaker now'. Or, 'Today was not so good'. The Namboodiris stood on the veranda eagerly listening to the bulletin. They then went indoors to inform the antharjanams.

The women were very anxious and fearful though Unni's own mother did not quite realize the seriousness of the situation. But Amma was well aware of the outcome of this disease. It was believed that this illness was Goddess Bhadrakali's doing, so Amma took a vow to propitiate the deity at the Kali temple at Kannenkavu. A twin set of mundus dyed red in the water in which the bark of the *chappanga* tree was boiled and cooled, was offered to the goddess. The branches of this tree were the ones used to make the sticks with which drums were beaten. In addition to this daily offering, Amma also arranged for the deity to be garlanded with hibiscus flowers.

Nobody spoke of the illness, though they thought of nothing else. I can still remember the fear and anxiety that gripped the illam at the time. People spoke in low voices and, when Amma could not control herself, she would say under her breath, 'I wonder how Unni is doing'.

Everyone was concerned about the patient.

The family did not sleep much at night, though we children dozed at intervals only to wake up with a start. It was on one such occasion that we were unnerved by a knock on the outer door early in the morning. An irikkanamma opened the door to a caregiver who brought the message: 'Tell them that it is all over'. He walked away and I can still recall the shock that his dark silhouette and frightening face inspired in us in the dim light.

I am not sure how Unni's last rites were performed because those who were claimed by this disease were not given the usual funeral. The caregivers must have buried the body. But we observed mourning for ten days and did not celebrate Onam which fell during this period.

I was six or seven years old when Unni died. I would have been in school but, at that time, we girls were not given formal education though our servants, Atti and Itti, Ichiripennu's granddaughters, went to the local school run by Muslims. But they did not speak of what they learned there. Even when we played together, there was no talk of school.

The image of the school assumed frightening proportions in my mind quite unexpectedly when I heard that some people had gone there to vaccinate the children against smallpox. It seems these people entered the classroom unannounced, shut the outer doors, and forcibly vaccinated them. Our servants' daughters came home scared and in tears, and showed us the round marks on their hands. We were terrified and congratulated ourselves on not being school goers.

The following day, after breakfast, we had started playing as usual when we heard our servants and stewards calling out to our irikkanammas, 'Ammaray, bring all the children out here'. We who had heard about the events at school began to cry. The women picked us up but we were terrified and tried to escape. They carried us, scratching and pinching, past the dining block and other parts of the house and lined up near the pathayappura.

The medicines and the spirit lamp were placed on a seat on the veranda. There were two of them and one held me tight and swabbed two points on the upper portion of my right arm with cotton. Then he sprinkled some medicine on the spots with an instrument like a wire. Finally, he pressed the wire hard and twisted it. I still remember how I cried out in fear and pain.

The lines of children went back and the irikkanammas applied the juice of some green leaves on the cuts. They must have felt that being vaccinated meant going against God's will. The circles did not fester, nor did they leave a mark. On that day, all the men and children of the illam were vaccinated. But the antharjanams were exempted because they could not allow themselves to be seen by other men, let alone be touched by them. When, later, I read N.S. Madhavan's description of a vaccination episode in his story, 'London Batheriyile Luthiniyakal', these memories were brought alive again.

But smallpox was not completely eradicated from the illam.

There was an antharjanam called Kankammayi in our illam. She was very close to Amma. Kankal was a shortened form for Kavunkal illam. She was the fourth wife of Achan's uncle. At one time, there were no menfolk in Kavunkal illam and only a mother and her daughter had survived. Achan's uncle married that girl and moved in with them because of an understanding that the bride's family would give him all their wealth. In return, they expected him to stay in their house. He had a child by her. Later, he married three others according to the practice of the day. This ammayi was the last of his wives, a young girl married to a man of sixty-five. Her husband died soon after and she had no children. She became Achan's aunt by marriage and forged ties of affection with Amma.

Ammayi knew how to please Amma, taking care to see that she did not annoy her. She was able to read her mind and act accordingly—even to the extent of walking northwards if Amma did so and sleeping on her side if Amma did. When it came to managing the house, Amma trusted Ammayi more than anyone else.

If ammayi wanted something, Amma got it for her. Ammayi had an overwhelming desire—to sleep on a mattress. At that time, it was uncommon for antharjanams to sleep on cotton-filled mattresses. There was only one mattress in the house and that was in the upstairs room used by the eldest Namboodiri. Only the wife whose turn it was to sleep with him had the good fortune to share the mattress. Otherwise, antharjanams and the children slept on a reed mat with a blanket and a mundu covering it. All illams had a stock of mats with frayed edges: shabby, faded blankets which they also shared with guests.

Ammayi nursed her desire for a mattress for a long time and, in the end, Amma helped her to get one. She had it made with the best cotton available in places like Varavur. Ammayi was overjoyed and, as she spent more and more time in Kankal, took the mattress with her.

On one of her visits to Kankal, we heard she had developed high fever and that it was diagnosed as smallpox. Her whole body had erupted with pustules and everyone at Kankal had left the house. This news shocked us all.

She was a woman, wasn't she? So ... only women could look after her and the caregivers happened to be Nairs. This was not the norm but Amma decided to overlook it. She gave them all they needed to nurse Ammayi and sent them with the instructions that they were to stay till the end, either way.

Many old mundus were needed to spread on the mat for the patient to lie on because these had to be changed when the pustules burst and soiled the sheet. Additionally, soft thin mundus were required by the caregivers to wrap around their fingers to remove the phlegm from the patient's throat. They also needed coriander seeds which were crushed, tied in a cloth, and soaked in water. The eyes were held open periodically and drops of this water used to clean them. Yet another requirement was broken rice to make gruel to be fed to the patient drop by drop. The caregivers also ate this gruel.

When these women reached ammayi, she was lying on her mattress refusing to move. Finally, she gave in to much persuasion and, leaving her coveted mattress, fell back on the mat, glaring angrily.

Time passed and there was no news from Kankal. At last, the caregivers returned after fifteen days with the news that it was all over. Kankalammayi was the last of my relatives to succumb to that dreaded, unnamable disease.

20 The Winds of Change Reach Mookkuthala

Although our desire to learn further and explore the world of ideas more deeply was fulfilled in a small measure, the practices at our illam were largely conservative and the general outlook, rather narrow. The situation in other illams in Mookkuthala was no different. However, strong winds of change had begun to blow within the Namboodiri community outside Mookkuthala. Although the transformation process had begun when I was only three years old, my sister's account of its early stages lingers in my memory.

On the way from our illam to Mookkuthala temple, there stood a madhom in a large compound. It belonged to Kanjoor Mana which owned vast areas of agricultural lands. The madhom was built so that the family could supervise agricultural work or use when they visited the temple.

It was in 1931 ... I still remember the event ... one evening, many Namboodiris and antharjanams, some forty to fifty in all, assembled at the madhom. The antharjanams had studs in their surgically shortened earlobes and wore blouses. The Namboodiris had cut off their *kuduma* or traditional tufts of hair and wore shirts and mundus.

* Translated by Radhika P. Menon

Our maids conveyed this information to the antharjanams at the illam and all of them were alarmed. How could they go to the temple the next day? That was their worry. Some antharjanams who came to Pakaravoor the same day, also spoke of the blouse-clad women they had seen: 'If they see us, they'll ask us to join them. We may agree and then we'll be obliged to remain with them!' The question that arose then was: how could the girls be sent to the temple? Breaking the practice of daily worship was simply unthinkable. Finally, a solution emerged: take a detour to reach the Mookkuthala temple. There was a circuitous road that passed Erkkara Illam gates. It meant a very long walk but wasn't the danger lurking in the usual route very grave? All the mothers and children moved in a close group along the road and took the same route back. I was carried all the way by a maidservant.

But on return, Unnikkali Edathi and two others lingered behind. They decided to take the usual road that went past Kanjoor madhom. Though afraid, they were curious to know what was taking place there. However, on reaching the madhom, they remembered what the antharjanams had said the previous day and, feeling even more nervous, walked faster along the path.

Wonder of wonders! Exactly as had been expected and described, a

woman stood in their path! Draped in a sari and wearing a blouse, her once-long earlobes had been surgically shortened and studs shone in them. She had cut her hair short in a style that is in vogue today. The very person, described by the antharjanams, now stood right in front of them. Edathi and her friends began to quake.

As they were about to run, the lady smiled and blocked their way. 'Wait a minute ... take this with you ... please give it to everyone at the illam to read,' she said and handed over some printed pages to each of them. 'Now you may go,' she stepped aside and permitted them to leave.

Edathi and her friends wondered whether they should keep the mysterious papers or discard them. It was not possible to carry them around at the illam, at least not publicly. That would be a great crime. But how could they be thrown away? Curious to learn the contents, Edathi and her friends folded and hid the papers in their fists and sped to the illam.

On reaching home, their fear, instead of abating, only intensified. What if someone saw the papers? Where could they hide them? If detected, things were likely to get completely out of hand and, worse still, they would lose the papers. So screwing up the sheets into a tighter ball, each of them tucked it away safely in the folds of her mundu. Concealing it was not enough. Wasn't the paper meant to be read? But there was just no privacy in the illam. Finally, they decided on the bath house. In the evening, when it was deserted they went to the bath house, carefully extracted the paper, unfolded it, and began to read slowly.

It was a letter to addressed to Namboodiri girls.

Dear Sister,

What a state you are in today! How many of you know that there is a world beyond the temple-pond of your *ammathu*, your mother's ancestral home? Do you have the freedom even to untie your hair-knot? Or part and comb your hair that stinks like decaying weeds from the pond? What about your education? I could argue that you would not even have tasted literacy if your father had not written the fifty-one letters of the alphabet on your tongue with his ring, the pavithramothiram, amidst the din of all those rituals in your childhood. Dear sister, think deeply and change yourself according to the times. Allow the rays of light to penetrate. Won't it be a great achievement if you manage to loosen at least one brick of that formidable fortress of orthodoxy? We will stand by you in all your difficulties. If we eat anything, you will get a share of it. Or shall we say, we will eat only after serving you. If we laugh, you will too. Rather, we will laugh only if you do.

Humbly yours

V.T. Bhattathirippad

Edathi and her friends read the letter several times. Tucking it back securely into the folds of their mundu, they returned to the illam. They did not understand much but felt an urge to go through it over and over again. The words stirred indescribable warmth in their hearts. Whenever they felt like reading it they went to the bath house, taking care to hide it properly before returning to the illam.

That flimsy paper soon began to tear with repeated folding and unfolding. In the course of time, it fell apart into shreds.

By the time I could read V.T. Bhattathiripad's letter to the girls, there was little left of it. Soaked through with their perspiration, the pamphlet had fragmented completely.

Looking back at it now, I think what took place at Kanjoor madhom was a sub-committee meeting of the *Yoga Kshema Sabha*. The Sabha held meetings at places where old Namboodiri traditions were most rigid. The assembly of forty-odd people at Kanjoor madhom was because Namboodiri orthodoxy had been more than commonly rigorous at Mookkuthala. The lady who gave Edathi that pamphlet must have been Arya Pallom. She was one of its prominent activists and wore her hair short.

That meeting may have lasted one or two days. It concluded with a community feast with the Namboodiris and the lower caste people eating together at the same table.

Three of my brothers—Neelakantan, Chithran, and Vasudevan—who unfailingly did their evening worship under the iron rule of apphan Namboodiris, also participated in the meeting and the communal lunch without seeking anyone's permission. Nor did they inform anyone. On

hearing this news, the apphan Namboodiris were beside themselves with fury and did not permit them even to step into the portico.

My brothers could sleep in the pathayappura but they were not to eat with the other Namboodiris and thus cause pollution. In short, my brothers were excommunicated. My Valiyamma's sons took the lead in supporting the apphans. They also scolded Amma for not keeping her sons in check. My brothers stayed at the pathayappura like outcastes, neither touching anyone nor entering the naalukettu. But soon, there was an astonishing phenomenon: one by one, they began to disappear! First, Neelakantettan, next, Chithrettan, and last, Vasudevettan.

The apphans remarked sarcastically, 'All of them have run away, God knows where!'

They had not run away; instead, left the illam to join school. Neelakantettan joined a school at Kumaranalloor; Chithrettan and Vasudevettan, another one in Ponnani. Thus, without seeking permission from their guardians, they began their formal studies.

21 *Doctor*

As a child, the only doctor I had ever seen was Dr Krishna Iyer who occasionally visited Pakaravoor from Trichur. Years later, his influence transformed the lives of the Namboodiris and ours, the antharjanams.

The doctor usually arrived when one of the Namboodiris fell ill. The practice was to try ayurvedic remedies and the allopathic doctor was called in only when this first line of treatment proved ineffective. The family steward would be sent with the details of the affliction in the morning and he would return with the doctor in the evening.

Krishna Iyer was a pleasant man of about fifty, neither fair nor dark-skinned, and of a proportionate build. He probably arrived in a motorcar, but I never saw it. I only remember him, dressed in a *mundu* and a shirt, coming up the steps of the illam, and walking in through the entrance.

The doctor carried the medical bag himself and placed it on the veranda while the Namboodiris stood up respectfully to greet him on arrival.

Anyone who wanted to enter the illam had to have a bath first. So he was given a towel to wrap around the waist after removing his dhoti and shirt. A Namboodiri would accompany him, carrying a laundered mundu and a *konakam*, a loincloth. The doctor would change into these after a bath and return with a wet towel draped across his shoulders.

* Translated by Indira Menon

The examination of the patient—always a man—followed. The doctor would go into his room, talk to the patient for a long time, and examine him with a stethescope. This would take almost an hour. Then he would emerge and sit on the veranda, eat snacks and drink coffee. Afterwards, he would write down the prescription and give it to the steward who would go to either Trichur or Kunnamkulam on the following day to buy the medicines.

The doctor visited only when the men fell ill. He was not sent for when the women were indisposed. Nobody paid much attention when women were unwell. In the absence of any specific illness in her old age, a vague reference was made to the effect that the woman had taken to her bed. She was confined to the vadakke ara and treated by well-known *vaidyans*—indigenous physicians—brought up in the tradition of their forefathers. Since women were not allowed to see men other than family members, the vaidyan would stand leaning against the door and would not venture close enough to either touch the patient or even to observe her symptoms, confining himself to asking her in loud tones what the problem was. The treatment depended on her answer or on the reply of those who stood near her.

If a birth was complicated, a doctor could be sent for. This happened with Amma during the delivery of my Valiyettan. She was in labour for three days and there was still no sign of the baby emerging. It was then decided to send for a doctor. The nearest doctor was in Palakkad, about fifty miles away. The steward walked to Palakkad and, by the time he and the doctor were half way home, the birth was over. A servant was sent with the message and the doctor returned to his clinic. But such cases were rare and, in general, doctors' visits were confined to the men of the household. There was an instance when a sick woman in the vadakke ara had bled heavily. It may have been cancer. The vaidyan came as usual, leaned against the door, asked questions, and prescribed the treatment. I do not recall whether she experienced any relief.

Dr Krishna Iyer came often to treat the Namboodiris from other illams as well. He observed the rules and, because he was a Brahmin, there was no fear of being defiled either. Therefore, in most illams, the word 'doctor' soon became synonymous with Krishna Iyer.

I had seen the doctor many times during this period but we, women, got to know him only several years later ... and that, too, for a totally different reason.

During my growing-up years, elongated earlobes, hanging right down to the shoulder, were considered beautiful. Round disc-like gold ear-rings—*chittu*—dangling from these earlobes and moving rhythmically, were thought to add to a woman's attractiveness.

The widening and stretching of the earlobes was a tortuous process. This began when the girl was eight and well before she was considered mature enough to wear underclothes, her ears were pierced, usually by the father. The earlobes were first smeared with butter and a sharp, pointed thorn was used to puncture them. A piece of fresh turmeric was attached to the end of the thorns which were left in place in the holes. In two days' time, the holes would be big enough for these to be removed and for thicker ones to replace them. This would be repeated several times and, as the days passed, the thorns would make way for light, round wooden earrings. The holes would grow larger and the girl would remain in agony. When she cried out in pain, the mother would console her, saying that this would make her look more beautiful. Even before the ears were pierced, the father would begin the ceremony with a prayer to Ganapati that the earlobes should grow long.

It took three or four months for the girl's earlobes to reach the right length. Every illam had a stock of these smooth wooden ornaments for use in this beautifying process. I remember that a number of them were stored in wooden containers and placed in the niche above the doors in Pakaravoor.

The wooden ear ornaments were replaced by gold discs when the girls got married. These and a thaali cluster on a string were given by the bridegroom's family to the bride as the customary gifts at the time of the wedding.

The elongated earlobes served yet another purpose. They came in handy when the Namboodiris got angry with their wives. I know of one who tugged at his wife's earlobe savagely and tore it because she was a little late for the regular *homam*. This was a much-talked about incident at that time.

A major social change that I witnessed between the mid-1930s and 1945 when I passed from childhood to early youth, was the elongated earlobe going out of fashion as a sign of beauty. Young Namboodiris now wanted their wives to stitch up their earlobes and wear normal sized earrings. This coincided with the time when the younger sons of Namboodiri households also began to get married. The men removed their tufts of hair and cut it short, and shirts came into fashion. They insisted that their wives should move out of isolation, discard their umbrellas and all-enveloping wraps, and wear saris and blouses instead. Gradually, the women, too, veered to the idea that smaller earlobes were beautiful.

But how were they to be made smaller? The answer came from the doctor I'd heard of when I was a child: Krishna Iyer of Trichur.

By the end of the 1930s, the doctor's hospital had become a regular visiting place for Namboodiris and antharjanams. Newly married men brought their wives to have their earlobes stitched. The procedure took only an hour. The doctor would cut the long earlobes, stitch them up, apply medicine, and cover them with cotton. On their return a month later, the doctor would himself pierce their ears and put in the earrings they had brought with them.

I was married in 1943 and had long earlobes at the time though, for some reason, they did not grow to the usual length and touch my shoulders. Still, they were longer than needed for earrings.

My husband Ravi Namboodiri believed that the earlobes should not be elongated. I thought so too and, two months after our wedding, we went from Nilayamgode in Chathanoor to Krishna Iyer's hospital in Trichur. There were already three couples waiting and our turn came after theirs.

The doctor had not changed much. He examined my earlobes and decided that there was no need to cut them because they were not too long. The holes had only to be filled. When I went back after a month, he pierced my ears and put in the earrings I had carried with me. We returned to Nilayamgode, very happy.

A long time before this, women social workers like Arya Pallom and Parvati Nenminimangalam had already had their earlobes shortened and had started to wear earrings. My husband's elder brother's wife, Parvati Nilayamgode, had also joined them. But my own elder sisters discarded their ear discs and had their earlobes stitched back to normal size only later.

This move proclaimed the birth of the new woman, one with normal-sized earlobes and dressed in a sari and a blouse. The hour-long surgery in a hospital in Trichur facilitated this evolution and the person heralding the revolution was the doctor I had seen since childhood—Krishna Iyer. With this development, he, who in the past had touched only the men's lives, began to exert his influence on ours as well.

22 *Marriage*

My wedding took place when I was fifteen. However, I learned of it only two days before it happened.

Usually it was the maid who informed the girl, maybe on their way to the pond for the evening bath, '*Kuttikkave*, it is your *manerichil* tomorrow'. Manerichil literally means 'leaving the *mana*' or 'shifting from one's house'. The servant invariably had no idea about either the groom or his house and the bride herself found out only after the ceremony.

It was Thankam, my English teacher, who told me about my wedding. '*Kuttikkave*, your wedding has been fixed for the day after tomorrow. So your tuitions will end tomorrow.' She sounded sad. However, she knew nothing about the groom. Thus, two years after puberty, I was given away in marriage. During this entire period, my life had been confined to the illam. A girl who had come of age was not supposed to step out of the illam or even see the portico. There was a pond near the kitchen exclusively for the use of an antharjanam. She could go there for her bath, but had no freedom to step beyond that limit. She could not attend any social function at other illams. A portion of the feast prepared on the

* Translated by Radhika P. Menon

occasion was brought to her. She was not permitted to attend any wedding ceremony—not even that of her siblings'. In those days, there were two or more grown-up girls in most Namboodiri families, who continued to stay at the parental illam, unmarried till the age of twenty-five or thirty, because their families could not afford dowries. I remember some illams near Pakaravoor where girls were still unwed at even thirty and thirty-two. And it was not unusual for some poor fathers to sell their daughters to unknown men in the name of marriage. I was almost a witness to one such tragedy.

An antharjanam, who cooked at our illam, had two daughters. Both lived with their father in their tharavadu. One day, a woman came to Pakaravoor and told her, 'Your daughter's wedding has been fixed for tomorrow. You must come home immediately'. The antharjanam left the very same day. On reaching home, she found a visitor there, apparently a Brahmin. Her husband told her that the man was a Namboodiri from north Kerala and had come to marry their elder daughter. The visitor's language was difficult to understand. As the wedding was to be conducted at the groom's illam, the father left with the stranger, taking his daughter along. He, however, returned after seeing the girl off at the railway station. The Brahmin had given him some money. The mother must have wept bitterly when she gradually realized that there was no wedding and that, having no dowry to give, the father had actually 'sold' their daughter to the man from Mangalapuram.

She never saw her daughter again. ...

There were several such stories and, in comparison, I believe my marriage was a blessing.

I learned about my husband and his illam only after the post-marriage ritual of kudiveppu. He was Ravi Namboodiri of Nilayamgode Illam, a great feudal family in Chathanoor in Palakkad district. They were Rigvedis. Besides, Nilayamgode had an *othu* school where the Vedas were orally taught to a very large number of students. My husband studied the Vedas under his father and also received training in othu. He had studied up to the eighth standard but was more interested in agriculture and skilled in all kinds of mechanical work. In fact, he personally supervised all the farm activities of Nilayamgode. Machines and technical subjects fascinated him—an unusual interest among Namboodiris in those days. This flair led him to learn driving. He even went to Coimbatore, bought a car, and drove it all the way to Nilayamgode. And it was he who carried out any repairs the car needed. When some Muslim youths in the neighbourhood complained of lack of employment opportunities, he set up a *beedi* manufacturing unit in a vacant plot and helped them eke out a living. The unit was named 'Jai Hind'. His elder brother Neelakantan Namboodiri was a prominent teacher of othu. Even while following all the Namboodiri rites at the illam, he involved himself in social activities.

They were the sons of Ittiravi Somayajippad, a well-known Kathakali artiste. There was absolutely no orthodoxy in this tharavadu.

I was lucky to marry into a family that held liberal views. Before the wedding, there is a ceremony called *Ayani oonu*. After an elaborate oil bath, the bride lights the traditional lamp and has a splendid lunch, somewhat similar to a birthday repast. Many married women attend this function but widows have no place there. Henna was applied on my hands, several silver rings were slipped on to my fingers, and I was taken to a room. That was usually the time when the bride was instructed on how to conduct herself at her husband's house. 'Nangayya, go and tell her what to do,' Amma said. Nangayya Edathi, Achan's niece, then advised me in detail on how to endear myself to everyone at my husband's house.

The wedding took place the next day. It was a simple affair in comparison with Achan's eldest daughter's marriage, which had been celebrated on a grand scale. Four days of ceremony followed and, on the fourth day, after a ritual bath, I was taken to Nilayamgode Illam.

A special bus was arranged for the trip—a rare phenomenon, considering the general conditions in 1942. Nilayamgode was roughly twelve miles from Pakaravoor. We reached there at about ten in the morning.

The bus pulled up at the gate of Nilayamgode and we had to walk to the illam. Just as all of us crossed the gate, my husband and I were asked to stop. Two people walked towards us and put red garlands around our necks. It was Sarojini, my husband's niece who garlanded me and Kizhakkedathu Namboodiri, a neighbour, who thus welcomed my husband. Almost immediately, all the Namboodiris assembled there shouted '*Inquilab Zindabad*' three times. That was the first time I heard the Communist slogan. I did not understand what the words meant or why they were being said.

Much later I realized that many members of the Yoga Kshema Sabha had joined the Communist Party. They were the ones who shouted the slogan which meant 'Long live the revolution!'

My relatives from Mookkuthala, not understanding a word and utterly baffled, simply stared at what they saw.

23 Kuriyedathu Thaatri

Surely the name that my generation heard most often was that of Kuriyedathu Thaatri. During my childhood, I too heard this name spoken frequently, but always in hushed voices. It was after my wedding, at my husband's house, that I came to know more about Thaatri whose notorious *smaarthavichaaram* or trial took place in 1905, twenty-three years before my birth. Vedic teachers, artistes, Sanskrit scholars, the social elite were all implicated in the case and excommunicated. Even twenty-five to thirty years later, the storm raised by Thaatri's trial in the Namboodiri community had not died down.

The first time I heard Thaatri's name was in the conversations of antharjanams who, passing that way, stayed at Pakaravoor illam. They mentioned the name in low, frightened tones. Today when I look back, I wonder: didn't those poor antharjanams derive a mysterious sense of joy, satisfaction, and energy in repeating Thaatri's story endlessly? In their stories, Thaatri was always to blame. She was the fallen woman who had enticed and insulted great Namboodiris as well as Vedic teachers. But beneath the tone of accusation, I also detected a note of unconscious appreciation of Thaatri.

* Translated by Radhika P. Menon

It was from Paapthi Valiyamma of Nilayamgode that I heard about her again. Valiyamma had seen Thaatri, known her, and had even stayed at her illam. She had also had great regard for Thaatri till she heard about the trial.

Paapthi Valiyamma had come to Nilayamgode as a little bride of nine. When her husband passed away, she was only twenty-five and remained a widow for the next fifty years. She must have been around sixty-five or seventy when I came to Nilayamgode.

Paapthi Valiyamma was never tired of repeating the story of her wedding. She was a small girl and her uduthu thudangal had not even been performed. One evening, when she was engrossed in games, a few antharjanams came to her illam. It never occurred to her to enquire about the reason for their visit. The very next day, after a bath, she was forced to wear the upper cloth. She resisted it strongly and the antharjanams of the illam had to tie it around her waist. It was only a week since her recovery from typhoid which had left her bedridden for about a month. Her hair was closely cropped; her skin dry and scaly. The bath over, she was taken indoors for *ayani oonu*. The little Paapthi was stubborn in her demand, 'I don't want to wear any mundu. The loincloth will do'. But no one paid her any attention.

The next morning, the twenty-five-year-old groom, Neelalohithan Namboodiri, reached Paapthi's illam of Kaplingattu. The same day, after the wedding, Paapthi was brought to Nilayamgode and the kudiveppu was performed. She looked like a scarecrow—all skin and bones and nearly bald. There were many girls of the same age at Nilayamgode and so Paapthi spent all morning in their company, playing games. She was terribly frightened of her husband and refused to sleep with him. The matrons of the illam had to take her by force to the bedroom upstairs. And, as soon as the door was opened in the morning, she escaped. Paapthi was not tall enough to unlock the door herself and had to wait for her husband to wake up and open it. She was fifteen or sixteen when she lost her fear of her husband.

My father-in-law, Ittiravi, was Valiachan Neelalohithan Namboodiri's youngest brother. He was a famous Kathakali artiste and Thaatri was one of the *sahridayas* who enjoyed his performances greatly.

K.P.S. Menon has written at length about the actor Ittiravi Namboodiri in *Kathakalirangam*. In those days, Namboodiris did not usually take part in Kathakali. They only enjoyed watching performances. The dance required great effort and was so fatiguing that the actors had to take sips of water in between. But this was taboo for Namboodiris because the Nair men, while applying their make-up, invariably touched them and thus caused a state of pollution. For such and similar reasons, Namboodiris did not like to perform Kathakali. But my father-in-law was so keen on performing this dance that he started learning it rather late, although he had completed his samaavarthanam and othu training by then.

K.P.S. Menon says that Ittiravi Namboodiri had his debut performance at the age of twenty-six. Paapthi Valiyamma was not very sure about the age. What she remembered was that my father-in-law had run away from the illam to train in Kathakali. Kaavungal, the ancestral house of many famous Kathakali artistes, was in Thichoor, close to Nilayamgode. My father-in-law stayed there and studied Kathakali under Kaavungal Kunjikrishna Paniker, the uncle of the famous Kaavungal Sankara Paniker (Sankara Paniker, later implicated in the Thaatri case, was of my father-in-law's age. He was born in 1873 and my father-in-law, in 1867). As Kaavungal was a Nair household, my father-in-law did not have his lunch there but went to the oottuppura attached to the Thichoor Ayyappa temple. Within two years of rigorous training, his fame began to spread. K.P.S. Menon has written admiringly about his handsome looks and consummate acting skills.

Valiyamma had heard that my father-in-law was most sought after for his role as 'Azhakiya Ravanan'. He performed this role regularly at the annual festival of Thichoor temple. Both during her husband's lifetime and later, Valiyamma occasionally went to her illam at Kaplingattu. On the way, as was the practice with the other antharjanams of Nilayamgode, she stopped at Kalpakamcheri, Kuriyedathu Thaatri's native illam. Chemmanthitta Kuriyedathu was Thaatri's husband's illam.

Valiyamma and Thaatri must have been of the same age. Even in her childhood, Valiyamma had heard about Thaatri. She liked Thaatri's hospitality, beauty, and friendly manner. One night, while resting at Kalpakamcheri, Valiyamma was astonished when she heard Thaatri reading the Ramayana in a melodious voice. In those days, very few girls in the Namboodiri community had such skills. At around that time, Valiyamma's husband Neelalohithan Namboodiri passed away. They had no children but as the family line had to go on, it was decided that Ittiravi Namboodiri should marry immediately. Many horoscopes were examined. Valiyamma remembered having eagerly insisted that Kalpakamcheri Thaatri's horoscope too be considered. But by then, Thaatri's horoscope was found to match with Kuriyedathu's.

However, my father-in-law had a sambandham at Kaavungal. It must have been Sankara Paniker's sister, who had even borne him a son. Meanwhile, his wedding was being planned at the illam. As he was always in the company of Kathakali actors, he had virtually been excommunicated by the Namboodiri community but he showed no inclination to leave that field. On everyone's insistence, however, he had to yield and also promise never to wear the Kathakali costume again. Thereafter, he became a householder and a little later, a Somayaji.

Years went by. One day, news about Thaatri's smaarthavichaaram broke out. When the names of some Kathakali performers were also mentioned along with those of other culprits, fear gripped the inmates of Nilayamgode Illam. Stories began to circulate about how Thaatri used to go to Thichoor temple to watch my father-in-law's performances and how, as a well-informed woman, she often sent him messages containing instructions regarding his acting and so on. Immediately, several kinds of pujas were conducted and many votive offerings made to the gods at the illam to prevent Thaatri from mentioning my father-in-law's name unjustifiably. Fortunately, Thaatri did not mention the name Ittiravi and everyone was relieved.

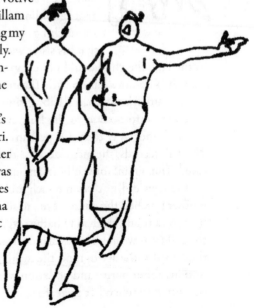

This trial destroyed Valiyamma's good impression about Thaatri. Perhaps this was because her brother Narayana Bhattathiri was one among the sixty-five names that Thaatri mentioned. Narayana Bhattathiri was a famous Vedic scholar. Thaatri, who had slept with prominent Vedic teachers of the community, famous artistes, and powerful men, had preserved a meticulous record of the date, zodiac sign, and day of her liaison with each of them. It seems she had even jotted down, in palm leaf documents, details about their birthmarks. Had she foreseen that these bits of information would one day come to her rescue and provide valuable evidence?

I vividly recall being a direct witness to some of the traumas and tragedies that Thaatri's revelations brought in their wake. One of my relatives, a Namboodiri from Okeel Mana at Chemmanthitta, was accused and excommunicated.

He was my maternal grandfather's brother-in-law. Okeel Mana was situated near Kuriyedathu. After his name was mentioned by the *saadhanam*, literally meaning 'object' or 'thing' as the erring antharjanam was called, he was forbidden entry to his illam. My grandfather immediately went to Okeel and brought his sister back home to Naripetta Illam. Such a move was legally permissible. A Namboodiri may be excommunicated but that ignominy did not apply to his wife. However, on reaching Naripetta my grandfather came to know that his sister was pregnant. There was a cruel clause in the law: the child could not escape its father's fate if it was conceived after the infamous liaison with Thaatri.

The antharjanam had a baby girl in due course. My grandfather conveyed the information to the king and the *smaarthan*. I think the trial was still underway then. Or perhaps it had just ended. After consulting Thaatri's records, the judge decreed that the child had to be excommunicated. Thus an infant was born an outcaste.

The laws did not permit such a child to live with its mother. If the mother touched the child—even to suckle it—she had to take a purifying bath. As a result, she had to bathe several times every day. However, when the child was weaned, it was denied its mother's caresses. Until her uduthu thudangal at the age of nine, the maids took care of her. But the primitive notions about purity and pollution were so rigid that even they were not permitted to touch her thereafter.

If a Namboodiri is excommunicated at birth, he becomes a *Chakyar*. An outcaste antharjanam becomes a *Nangyar*. Thus the unfortunate child born to my grandfather's sister became a Nangyar. When she was six months old, a Nambiar came to Naripetta, whispered the word 'Nangemma' into her ears, and put a few grains of cooked rice in her mouth. This simple ritual transformed a tiny Namboodiri girl into a Nangyar.

The seventy years that Nangemma Nangyar spent at the illam must have been lonely and unbearably sad. On reaching a marriageable age, perhaps realizing that it was difficult to find a groom from the already dwindling Chakyar community, that wise lady opted to remain single.

I distinctly remember seeing this Nangyar when she accompanied her mother (my grandfather's sister) to Pakaravoor, on their way to Mukkola temple. The daughter was not permitted to enter the naalukettu of the illam.

There were many such Nangyars in the vicinity of Kuriyedathu illam. K.B. Sreedevi's novel *Yagnam* tells the tale of one such Nangyar.

I have heard another similar story of a personal tragedy that was triggered by Thaatri's smaarthavichaaram. On seeing that the trial showed no signs of ending even after Thaatri's mention of sixty-five names, the distraught king ordered the smaarthan and others to wind up the case. Yet the saadhanam did not lose her composure. It seems she concluded saying, 'My younger aunt will list the rest of the names,' much to the discomfiture of the smaarthan and the interpreters of the law. The younger aunt, a widowed middle-aged antharjanam at Chemmanthitta, was Thaatri's husband's aunt.

This declaration made it impossible for the smaarthans to let the aunt go unexamined. They tried their best to collect evidence from her but nothing was forthcoming. Nevertheless, they lacked the courage to exempt her and retain her within the community. The final verdict was a kind of life-imprisonment. She had to remain confined to a building, north of Chemmanthitta Illam, with no right to touch even her maids. For the rest of her life, she had no one for support and survived solely on the rations of food the servants left for her.

In my childhood, I heard some visiting antharjanams describe the aunt's last days: 'It seems she died in that building ... she is indeed lucky ... didn't suffer much, after all'.

The bond between Nilayamgode and Kalpakamcheri Illams came to an end with Thaatri's trial. In the course of time, Kalpakamcheri Illam fell to ruins. The same fate overtook Kuriyedathu Illam. By the time of my wedding, Kalpakamcheri Illam was already reduced to its foundation stones. One day, when we were passing that way, Paapthi Valiyamma showed me what was left of Thaatri's illam.

I stayed at Nilayamgode Illam for only about a decade. Paapthi Valiyamma died and, after the family partition, we bought a small house near Thichoor temple and shifted residence. Our house was situated beyond the western gate of the temple and the adjoining pond. It was on a stage erected beneath the banyan tree near this gate that Kaavungal Kunjikrishna Paniker and his students, my father-in-law, and his contemporary Kaavungal Sankara Paniker, had performed Kathakali. And it was in the bath house attached to this temple pond that Thaatri had sought to make love to Kaavungal Sankara Paniker while he was still in the *'Keechaka'* costume, she had admired so much. Sankara Paniker, eventually excommunicated after the trial, had to leave the region never to return.

For a long time, that small bath house remained intact but gradually, it fell apart. Today, the building no longer stands. What remains are only a few huge bricks which once formed its foundation. They lie scattered here and there like the last letters that bring a grand story to its close.

24 *Fever*

I developed high fever after a trip to Trichur for the annual celebrations of the Namboodiri school where Kamala, my brother-in-law's daughter, was a student. The festivities had lasted till the morning hours with cultural programmes of music, dance, and drama keeping us awake all night. My active participation in the merrymaking must have exhausted me and so I was in a daze when I walked the three miles to Nilayamgode from the Vattolikkavu stop where we had alighted from the Trichur-Pattambi bus. I dragged my feet and paused to rest on the way, imagining that it was lack of sleep that caused my weariness.

What had started as a headache developed into a burning sensation all over. It was customary for those who returned from travel to have a bath before entering the house. But since in my condition a bath could be dangerous to my health, I was put in the building adjoining the water tank where people who were considered polluted were made to stay. It was thought at first to be a fever accompanying a cold and the family became anxious only when I collapsed after a giddy spell. By then I'd been ill for a week.

In the meantime, I was joined in my room by another person with fever. Our neighbours, a mother and daughter from Thekkattu *mana*, were our

* Translated by Indira Menon

guests because their illam was being renovated. Such mutual help and friendship was quite common at the time. When the daughter Arya who was of my age developed fever with similar symptoms, she was brought in to share my room.

After 1940, it was possible, though rare, to reach Allopathic practitioners. Orthodox Namboodiri homes where homam was conducted and the sacrificial fires burned, hesitated to permit doctors entry. They were afraid that these doctors who cut up dead bodies would pollute the illam. It was therefore not uncommon to find many children and otherwise healthy young people dying for want of medical care. The deaths of the two young sons (twenty-five and eighteen) of the antharjanam of Mangalatheri illam within a few hours of each other had caused deep concern at the time.

Most illams had a family doctor who was located in a town nearby. If someone was seriously ill, then the doctor was brought home. Gopalan Nair, who was the family doctor of Nilayamgode, treated me and Arya during our illness. To facilitate the examination, we were moved to an inner hall adjoining the entrance and the fever was diagnosed as typhoid. By then, my elder brother-in-law's son, Narayanan, had also contracted the fever and was confined to a room in the southern part of the house, the thekkupuram.

There were few medicines available then to control typhoid. We were very ill and the medicines took time to bring the fever down. It was considered more important to ensure that we did not become weaker. The doctor stressed the need for good nursing care. But even in such a critical state, nobody thought it necessary to transfer the patients to a hospital. Though there were hospitals in towns nearby, Namboodiris, especially the women, were rarely taken there. Our doctor, P.T. Gopalan Nair, worked in a government hospital in Trithala. He visited us in the evenings after his duty hours there. Since the doctor got angry if our room was not clean, an irikkanamma stayed with us all the time.

A chart was hung on our bedside, stipulating the timings for giving medicines and food. I lay on a low bed which women used after delivering a baby. Every three or four hours, our temperature was taken in a thermometer and entered in a chart. There were two people to nurse us. I was taken care of by Pindali amma, who was very close to us and cared deeply about us. Arya was nursed by her mother. My husband Ravi Namboodiri attended to Narayanan, his ettan's son.

Pindali Amma was a widow and, therefore, was not permitted to eat or even drink water before a bath. This was very inconvenient since she had to wait till after ten o'clock to go to the tank, conduct the *thulasi* and *saligrama puja* before drinking coffee. After lunch she'd sit by me again without any food or even water for the rest of the day. When my husband entered the room to take our temperature and give us medicines, Pindali Amma and Arya's mother would stay hidden behind the half-closed door in the adjoining room because it was improper to be seen by a man to whom they were not related. These antharjanams used the services of the irikkananmma to give my husband the current status of our illness.

The most complicated part of the nursing was to chart the course of the fever. Our attendants had no clue about how this was done. Therefore, my husband had the responsibility of recording the temperatures several times a day. He had to go up and down the stairs many times to give Narayanan his medicines and food at the designated time, but there were worse consequences. After every use, the thermometer had to be shaken well till the mercury went down before the next temperature could be taken. This frequently repeated action caused great strain to his right shoulder. Very soon he could hardly move his arm, but there was no one else who could take over this responsibility. His ettan had gone to Kuroor Namboodirippad's illam in Trichur to look after his elder son Ravindranathan, who was also down with fever. Ravindranathan was studying in the high school there.

The calm in the inner courts of the illam gave way to turmoil. The doctor visited regularly and, after examining the temperature chart, changed the dosage of the medicines when necessary. He reiterated that the patient had to be forced to eat, drink, and be medicated at the right time. He left after giving instructions for us to be rubbed down frequently with a towel dipped in warm water and to keep him informed if the temperature fluctuated abnormally. But, even with the best care, I was slowly losing consciousness. I lay in bed, half aware and delirious.

I had fallen ill the day after the annual celebrations of the Namboodiri Vidyalayam. Therefore, it was not surprising that, in my moments of delirium and partial wakefulness, the events of the day were uppermost in my mind. I would suddenly start singing '*Mada Mahisha Mangalam*' in a loud voice and repeat the spirited dialogues of the drama in weak tones. I would try to get up and replicate the dance steps, only to collapse on the floor. This made Pindali Amma so anxious that she refused to move from my side and sat with an arm placed on my body burning with fever. At night, she slept hugging me to her side in order to restrain sudden movements.

Paappi Valiyamma of Nilayamgode cared for me deeply. She was saddened to see me in this semiconscious state. She'd come close to the bed and bend down to look at me. Since she was an orthodox antharjanam for whom the ritual of the bath followed by prayers was inviolable, she could not touch me. Yet, her eyes would stroke me and offer comfort. I had arrived in Nilayamgode after my wedding just four or five months earlier, fair and quite plump with hair that reached my knees. Valiyamma now agonized over my darkened skin, wasted frame, and loss of hair. She mourned my impending death saying that she had not spent enough time with me. It became increasingly unbearable for her to see me in this condition. She feared that even if I escaped death, at least one of my senses—sight, hearing, or speech—would be affected forever.

Death was considered certain. The fever had started with me and so diagnosis was also delayed. Therefore, the medicines took their time to be effective. Arya, too, had high fever but she did not lose consciousness. On the other hand, Narayanan and Ravindranathan recovered fast, probably because they were children. At the same time, there was worrying news from Mangalore. Kamala had been down with fever for a week. She was staying with her uncle and doing her intermediate course in Mangalore after completing her tenth class from the Namboodiri school. On hearing this news, my brother-in-law left for Mangalore.

Amma arrived from Pakaravoor when she heard about the intensity of my fever. She spent two days with me. On Ekadashi day, Amma, who was a widow, fasted without even a sip of water. She was returning the next day to Mookkuthala. After my delirious ranting at night, she feared that she would not need to visit this house again. In the morning, she had a bath and went into the kitchen. She had fasted the previous day and so it was imperative that she eat or drink something before she left. It would bring bad luck to the family if she were to leave on an empty stomach after fasting on Ekadashi. Amma entered the kitchen and had taken only one sip of the coffee left by the fireside for another when she heard the sounds of someone falling in the kizhakkini, trying to control her sobs.

Soon, more people joined in the wailing saying 'Shiva, Shiva'. Amma must have put her glass down.

It was Kamala's mother, my sister-in-law, who had fallen unconscious in the kizhakkini. A telegram had arrived the previous night asking her to go immediately to Mangalore to see her daughter. Krishna Warrier, the manager at Nilayamgode, arranged for a taxi to take her to Mangalore. They left very early in the morning taking the baby Unni and Cherona, the irikkanamma, with them. From Pattambi they had to cross the river by boat. The boat had just moved from the *thekke kadavu* (southern banks) when one approached from the opposite direction asking them to return. It was Mozhikunnam Namboodiri, a close friend of the Nilayamgode family, who gestured to Krishna Warrier to turn back. My brother-in-law had sent him a telegram informing him of his daughter's death and asking him to stop anyone coming from Nilayamgode from proceeding further. The boat turned back and Krishna Warrier instructed Cherona to hold the antharjanam down. Mozhikunnam returned to Nilayamgode with them in the car. My sister-in-law ran out of the car into the kizhakkini and collapsed there.

Kamala was a dear friend, someone I had grown close to after just a short period of acquaintance. She had a wheatish complexion, a good figure, sparkling eyes, and a pleasant expression. Of all the children at Nilayamgode, she was the most energetic. Her death did not register in my mind for several days. It seems Amma had expected to hear the same news about her daughter when she left Nilayamgode. But my condition improved gradually and I learnt about my delirium from other people's tales. I have a photograph to remind me of my days of fever. In it, I had neatly cut short hair which had just started growing back after it had all fallen out during my illness. Even today, my grandchildren are fascinated by this photograph.

25 Harvest

In different phases of my life, I was a part of three villages which measured their wealth by paddy fields. Industries and factories had not set foot there. My home in Mookkuthala where I was born and grew up was on an island surrounded by breathtakingly beautiful backwaters. For nearly six months every year, I would lose myself in the rush of the overflowing waters, feeling it run through my hands, plucking water lilies, and rejoicing in the occasional water festivals.

At times, these spaces came to life with the loud singing of the men who turned the wheel with their feet while readying the water-filled fields for transplanting paddy. Though this shattered the peace of the night, for me, this tune sounded more like a lullaby. Later, oil engines replaced these men, their loud noise startling us even as we marvelled at them and continued to make such sounds a part of our nights.

Most of those who worked in the fields were Harijans. We, therefore, could not get a close look at them or learn how they lived. In the mornings when we were on our way to the temple, our irikkanammas walked alongside saying 'Yaa ... hey ... yaa ... hey' in loud tones. The street leading to the Naranipuzha bathing ghat dissected our path to the temple and we had to cut across it to be on our way. Sometimes, when the women field hands

* Translated by Indira Menon

strayed into our paths in their hurry to reach their
destination, they would flee as if they had com-
mitted a crime. I only have vague memories of
such faces filled with fear. A visitor to our illam remarked that it was difficult to distinguish
between a *cherumi*, a low-caste woman, a crow,
and a buffalo. They all looked so alike. This
was endorsed by the women in our family
who also considered them less than human.
They believed that the piled-up paddy in their
courtyard was their reward for worshipping
Bhagawathi and Cherukunnilamma every day.
But they refused to see the hard work that had
gone into such good harvests.

When I got married and went to my husband's home in Chathanoor,
there were no backwaters or rivers to be seen. Instead, there were vast
fields where virippu and mundakan were cultivated in the month of
Kanni. Several steps led up to the gate house from the west side, the
padinjarupuram of the nalukettu where the women lived. The cowshed,
the wall with the mud roof, and the hall where paddy was threshed with the
feet, all adjoined the gate house. Though it was a little removed, we could
still see the whole process of the paddy being tied into sheaves, threshed
with the feet, and the grains separated from the chaff by the wind. I was
fascinated by the sight which was quite new to me and watched it with
great interest.

The number of bullocks in the cowshed depended on the size of the
paddy fields. When the sheaves were threshed and the grains separated,
the stalks or hay were piled high near this space, trussed up with bamboos, and bound tightly together to protect them from the rain. This was
referred to as hay-stacking and was done only by those who were adept at
it. Everyday small quantities of hay were pulled out carefully to be fed to
the cattle. They were so bundled that each one held the required quantity
and also ensured that rain water did not penetrate them. Hay was strewn
in generous quantities for the cows and bullocks in their feeding troughs.
Cow dung was used as organic manure in the fields. The luxuriant green
leaves from large trees on the grounds were cut down and added to this as

manure. The soil received these instruments of renewal eagerly and waited with added vigour for the next transplanting of paddy.

Third, it was Trichur village which I claimed as my own which brought me close to the agricultural workers .... By then, untouchability had by and large been removed. It was an area with hills, endless forests, paddy fields, extensive open land.

In this, the third place I had made my own, we lived on friendly terms with the farm workers. Three of them—the head *Pulayan* Ayyappan, his wife Neeli, and sister Kali—had come with us to work here. They built their huts on the far side of the fields with four bamboo sticks holding up the four sides covered with coconut leaves. When it was being built, they stayed in a corner of the room where paddy was threshed. By nature hardworking, their sense of involvement and discipline was clear.

Neeli's children and mine were born almost at the same time and in the same year. I gave her the cloth to tie her child's cradle. Bananas dried and powdered for baby food were shared with her. When one of us fell ill, Neeli's concoction of medicinal leaves did us good. It also provided a panacea for the sickness of the villagers. Their care of their women post-confinement was unusual. They gathered all kinds of non-poisonous leaves from the forest, ground them into a paste, and cooked it into a porridge with rice to which turmeric and pepper were added. They did not have a long period of rest after their confinement and returned to work in the fields within fifteen days. They took pregnancy and childbirth in their stride. After a day's work harvesting paddy in the fields and threshing it with their feet at night, Neeli had been seen abruptly abandoning the sheaf under her feet and withdrawing into her hut. We'd be filled with wonderment to hear a baby's cries not long after that. I've heard that once Neeli emerged soon after childbirth to help with the harvesting when they were short of hands. People noted Neeli's presence only when the harvested sheaves grew quickly in number.

Such strenuous exertions ensured their good health. From early morning to late in the evening, their bodies were exposed to the sun's rays and the falling rain, giving them the strength to hoist heavy things. I've seen Neeli's daughter, Kalipennu, carrying a head-load of ten *paras* of paddy or a large bundle of green leaves which would normally have called for four people to transport. My heart ached for her especially because she was of the same age as my daughter.

There was a big demand for women who could harvest paddy at great speed and other landlords waited for Neeli to be free. Even when they had no work in our fields, they'd ask our permission before going to work for others. Neeli's postal address read: Nilayamgode Mana Neeli, Nellikunnu, Thichoor. At the beginning of the harvest, the right to place the first sheaf in the family courtyard belonged to the head *Pulayi*. When she entered the compound from the east, the *kizhakkupuram*, carrying a head load of sheaves from the first harvesting, the family matriarch would be ready after a bath to welcome her with a lighted lamp. The sheaf would then be lowered to the ground and the pulayi would withdraw after paying obeisance to Mother Earth and her produce, the paddy bundle. Soon after, other head-loads of paddy would follow in a queue.

Every family had its own field hands, but others participated too. When extra hands were not needed, the surplus was sent back. They were unhappy at this and left the field in tears.

Harvest time was a period of rejoicing for the children. Village schools reported low attendance at this time. Since most of the masters also had their own fields, their absence was considered a boon. The children helped out their mothers who harvested paddy in the fields. They would carry small bundles on their heads and arrange them on the threshing floor. Several ears of paddy tied together with a single spike were called 'churootu'. Each of these was bound even before they moved on to the next. Everyone had her own method of doing this. Neeli and Kali had a distinctive, identifiable method of tying the churootu. Children recognized this and made bundles accordingly before transporting them to the threshing floor, and before they returned to the fields they would drink a lot of water from a large covered vessel placed in the courtyard.

My children were reluctant to go to school because they were eager to be a part of the excitement. Realizing that books were not the sole repository of knowledge, we did not push them. They would walk about in the courtyard trying to assess whose bundles grew taller and wider than the others'. I still laugh at a story they told me when they were in high school. It seems that children who handed in leave-letters during this period would cite as their reason: 'I'm suffering from *Valiyapadam* field harvesting'.

It was during one such activity that news was received of the AEO* arriving for an inspection of the school. This was serious. The headmaster met with the farmers and decided to suspend harvesting the next day. When Krishnan Ezhuthchan 'master' made a decision, no one opposed it because the entire area respected him. All the children had a bath, wore clean clothes, and attended school. Such cooperation was a clear example of the general goodwill prevailing in the village.

Virippu and mundakan cultivation were done simultaneously and not one after the other. When virippu was nearly ready for harvesting, the seeds for the next season would be soaked and sprouted. By the time the harvesting was done and the soil readied to receive the next batch of seedlings, the sprouts would be a month old. The furrows for transplanting the sprouts would have been dug earlier. There was a certain ritual involved in soaking the seeds. The *pathaayam* was opened on an auspicious day, the man who went in sent up a silent prayer to the family deity and transferred three fistfuls of paddy to a basket. After this, the seeds were shovelled out to a large vessel filled with water. The chaff that rose to the surface was removed and the good seeds were tipped into a sunken bund with a base of wooden planks built in the courtyard. Long turmeric leaves were spread at the bottom and then the bund was filled with soaked paddy. The top was covered with the twigs broken off from the gooseberry tree. This was the season when the gooseberry trees were in flower and small gooseberries

* Assistant Educational Officer.

were forming in them. Banana leaves covered the top so that sunlight would not penetrate the bundle. Twice a day the banana leaves were removed to wet the seeds with the water brought in potfuls from the pond by women. On the third day, one of the men stepped into the bund and stirred the corn slightly before sprinkling the water mixed with cow dung handed to them by the women workers. The covered paddy sprouted the next day and was ready for transplanting. *Chitteli* seeds were the preferred ones for mundakan cultivation, whereas the seeds used for virippu cultivation, were *kattamodan*, *aryan*, and *thavalakannan*.

Even as the sprouted seeds were spread out on the veranda to remove excess water, farm hands prepared the field for the sowing. Sackfuls of these seeds were carried by women to the fields, taking care not to break the sprouted ends. The base was prepared to suit the requirements of rice cultivation on hillsides. Excess water was drained and the soil readied to hold the seeds firmly in place. The sowing itself had to be done quickly. The seeds had to be slid between the fingers so that they did not fall in a bunch in any one spot. It was a fascinating sight to see workers moving swiftly through the sodden earth holding a basket filled with seeds in one hand and a fistful of seeds in the other. The hands moved rapidly to deposit the seeds in their designated furrows.

After working in the fields, the women would come directly to our house. The sprouted paddy was heaped in a corner. This was the time to which my children and theirs looked forward with great excitement. They would look on impatiently while Neeli and others washed and cleaned the paddy several times over, made a fireplace with three stones, and lit it. They would then poured small quantities of seeds into a mud pot placed on the fire and stir it with a new broom made of stripped green spines of coconut leaves. When it was sufficiently roasted, they would transfer it into a tall stone mortar and start to pound it. The beat of several pestles pounding the paddy by turn and the delicious smells that rose from it seemed to envelop us. The sounds that rose from them as they pounded the paddy 'sh, sh' reverberated in various octaves. They showed no visible signs of fatigue after a gruelling day's work. The winnowed and cleaned *avil*, or beaten rice, had a reddish tinge and was mildly sweet. It would be transferred into a new basket and placed on the front veranda from where children would grab large quantities, still fragrant from being roasted. There would be enough and more for all of them. When darkness fell, they would return to their homes with their children, carrying lighted flares in their hands, a sackful of paddy as wages balanced on their heads, and a bundle containing avil slung from their shoulders. They seemed contented as they walked on the raised paths between the fields and climbed up towards Nellikunnu.

The workers' children stood guard over the planted seeds till they took root in the soil. Small birds like *kuriyatta* would pick up the seeds and fly away with them. The children ran around on the paths periodically making a noise with their tins and sticks. This was called shooing away the birds for which they were paid.

After the Kanni harvest, preparations would be afoot to get the fields ready for the next sowing. Cow dung, green leaves, and wood ash were used as fertilizer. In addition to what was available in our own compound, we also gathered all the green twigs and leaves that we could lay our hands upon. For this purpose, we had bought two acres of land and planted several trees in it, the main variety being the roseapple tree. It was believed that its leaves oozed a liquid which gave a new lease of life to the soil. The ploughed fields with standing water absorbed this organic matter in two weeks' time.

No man ever worked as a field hand, uprooting and transplanting the seedlings. This was a busy time for the women. Their joy in the work poured out in the form of songs even into our courtyard. Their songs, based on the heroic tales of Unniarcha and Kungi, helped them to over-come their weariness.

Neeli was an expert at transplanting the seedlings and she could do the work of two people. Bundles of uprooted seedlings would be scattered on all sides of the field for easy access when she had exhausted the seedlings in her hand. When harvesting was in progress, it was common to complete the transplanting as they moved backwards. Other landlords waited for Neeli to be free to work for them.

Even as this work was being done in the fields where mundakan was sown, the virippu seeds were dried and stored. It needed a lot of care to preserve the seeds and store them in the pathaayam. The seeds were labelled for identification by my children, who wrote the names down on paper and placed it in the sacks. During this period, the monsoons would not have retreated. The rain clouds would form a ring around the morning sun and threaten the seeds spread out to dry in the courtyard. Farmers' wives could tell from the direction of the clouds whether they would bring rain or not. Their forecast was seldom wrong. When the direction of the wind foretold rain, the women would run in from the fields even without being told, to shift the paddy to a dry place. When the paddy was almost dry, it would be taken out of the pathaayam and again exposed to seven days of sunshine and seven nights of dew.

After the mundakan seeds were sown, there was a period of rest till harvest time. When the sowing was done, a banana plant with its mature bunch of banana fruits would be uprooted from the landlord's compound and replanted in the path between the fields. The oldest field hand would circle the tree amidst loud cheers, cut down the bunch, and distribute it to all present. They then departed with more resounding cheers. The fish curry that was cooked in the pots and was their daily fare would give way to curried bananas on that day. While the women hurried to finish their cooking, the men went to the toddy shop with some paddy tied up in their mundus for payment.

Mundakan harvesting began when the Thiruvathira moon began to wax in the sky. Therefore, the nights were not quite as dark. We had a petromax which was a rarity in the place. Electricity came to our village much later. There were only two people who knew how to light the petromax and put it out—my husband and our steward, Vishwanathan. It was not easy to light this lamp. Children would gather around it as at a strange sight and wait patiently for it to burn. It was used on special occasions like weddings and temple festivals and only rarely for harvesting. The base of the petromax was made of steel, polished to a shine that reflected the children's faces in various distorted angles. This would be greeted with great hilarity. The lamps we usually lit struggled to dispel the darkness. They were small lanterns referred to as *pathinalaam* number (number fourteen), indicating their size. Children would be so excited to see the bright light of the petromax that they would be reluctant to go to sleep.

There were also those who thought that darkness was a blessing. When harvesting went on into the night, the harvested bundles would disappear before they reached our courtyard. Some stewards bullied the field hands and played such stealthy games to grow rich.

Daytime was spent harvesting paddy and the night, threshing it with the feet—this was how each day went. Grandfathers and grandmothers also arrived to help their children, carrying their food and mats for them to sleep on. We gave them pickles—*kadumanga* or *chethumanga*—to spice up their food. They spent the whole night in our courtyard, resting for a while on the mats and getting up again to work They helped by fanning the paddy to separate the chaff.

When the sheaves were brought from the fields, the scattered paddy was swept and placed carefully in a heap. These were fully ripened grains, excellent for use as seeds. Each day after the last sheaf was brought in, the scattered grain was piled up and this work was called '*kalodi*', sweeping the *kalam* or the threshing floor.

After the harvest, the hay heaped in a corner after the threshing was spread out in the courtyard to dry in the sun. The women stood in rows facing each other and holding long bamboo sticks in each hand. They moved forwards and backwards in unison, thrashing the hay to synchronized sounds. These movements were not unlike the Onakkali steps to the song '*Will you give me the girl, O trader?*' When they were done, they shook the hay and tied it in small bundles before fastening it on the bamboo fixed firmly in a corner of the compound. Grains which lay scattered in the courtyard were separated from the chaff and the paddy was made into rice. The chaff that still stuck to the grain was filled in a sack and taken to Pattambi to be sold. Fishermen ground this coarsely to use as bait. This was a benefit accruing in the balance sheet for working in the fields and was claimed exclusively by the women.

When paddy filled the granary and hay was stacked in the courtyard, Poothan and Thara entered the scene. With the start of the temple festivals, the field hands spent all their nights watching the festivities on the temple grounds. The whole family accompanied them with the women carrying head loads of paddy for sale at the fair. In normal circumstances grain obtained as daily wages was just sufficient for their needs. But immediately after the harvest, they had more than enough to spare and could afford to splurge. They returned from the fairgrounds with dates, roasted grain, *murukkus* to munch, and enough glass bangles to cover their wrists. When their funds were exhausted, they would not hesitate to take a loan against the following year's harvest.

Such celebration of the harvest is a rare sight in these times. Fields have been converted into large houses. People have moved from paddy cultivation to growing cash crops. Those who still grow paddy mourn their losses. Cases of farmers committing suicide are on the increase. Several causes such as the heavy expenses of cultivation, falling prices of food grains, increased imports, adverse weather conditions, and the complex laws of storage, have contributed to making farming an unviable option. The younger generations leave their villages looking for better job opportunities. Those who stay back are apprehensive about *anthaka vithu*, seeds lethal to cultivation. All over the world less and less paddy is being cultivated. But the Malayalis still consider rice their staple diet. Farmers are disheartened by adverse conditions such as scanty rainfall, severe summer, and inadequate water supply. The strong and weak points of paddy cultivation are related to water. The level of water is threatened when transplanting is affected. In Kerala, paddy cultivation not only aims at self sufficiency in food but also, more important, it helps in solving the ecological problem of conserving the water level. We can only hope that at least those who live in villages will revert to the healthy and profitable tradition of paddy cultivation.

26 Granary

Hide and seek was the favoured game during our childhood. Girls were allowed to join in till they were nine or ten years old, before they started wearing adult undergarments. This was an exciting and daring sport in which a large group of older brothers, sisters, and visiting children participated enthusiastically. There were many places to hide especially in the large nalukettu and *pathaayappura*. The darkness, silence, sheltered spaces, and the possibility of finding more such secluded spaces made the game very interesting. The wide hall above the store room entrance was one such hiding place with bunches of bananas both small and large hanging from rows of wooden bars on the ceiling.

The game started in the afternoons when the Namboodiris were resting after lunch in the pathaayappura and the antharjanams in the inner rooms. *Irikkanammas* would be busy emptying and cleaning the serving vessels and the estate managers would be stretched out on the veranda, enjoying the breeze from the west. The hall had four *pathaayams*, both large and small set against its four walls and raised two or three feet above the floor level. The smaller pathaayams held grains for daily use and also various pulses like millet, horse gram, green gram, wheat, sesame seeds, and peppercorns. The pathaayams were usually full. We hid in them,

* Translated by Indira Menon

taking time off to eat a banana and generally celebrating the afternoons. Our older brothers joined in on the rare occasions when they got time off from preparing themselves for the sacred thread ceremony. During this period, they were allowed to eat only three times a day and drinking water was forbidden. But once, whether out of hunger or curiosity or greed, one of my older brothers had just peeled a banana, preparing to eat it when Nambisan who was in charge of the storeroom came up the stairs. If Nambisan reported this, there would be an enquiry by the elders of the family followed by severe punishment and penance. Therefore, Ettan tried to swallow the banana whole even as he attempted to hide in a pathaayam. This particular one was three fourths full of millet, which were small smooth grains. So he sank into the grain heap when he jumped inside. He could not shout because the banana was stuck in his throat. But he held on to the edge of the pathaayam and my elder sister, who saw his hand on the rim, asked Nambisan to help him to come out. Nambisan did not report this incident. Instead, he blamed himself for having come upstairs at the wrong time.

Pathaayappura must have derived its name from pathaayam—a place where grain is stored. This building was separated from the main nalukettu by a courtyard. The ground floor of this building housed a large pathaayam with a veranda all around it and an entrance at one end. When you went up the stairs to the first floor, you came to another broad open veranda. There were doors to large halls leading from the veranda which were used as bedrooms by apphans, the second and younger-born Namboodiris, by young boys who had completed their upanayanam, by scholars of Sanskrit and house-guests. This was a place only for men. The large hall upstairs of the Pakaravoor pathaayappura held a wide collection of books and also doubled as the schoolroom for teaching Sanskrit.

The small pathaayams were situated above the entrance to the store-room just outside the pathaayappura. Some of these were also to be found in the thekkini inside the nalukettu. The western wing had a *machu* on the ground floor and a built-up pathaayam above it. The pathaayam inside the machu was filled with the golden grains of paddy. Below this were placed inverted golden coloured urulis and large vessels, all pointers to the prosperity of the family. If the machu was filled with paddy throughout the year, the family could heave a sigh of relief.

There were many kinds of pathaayams—large, small, built-in, pathaayam to store the seeds, box-like pathaayams, and pathaayam boxes. Of these, the pathaayam boxes were the smallest, easily moved around by a couple of men. When such pathaayams were brought to the door to be sold, the price paid was the quantity of paddy that it could hold. These were usually placed in the kitchen and their covered top provided a resting place for the antharjanams in the midst of their kitchen duties.

The daily requirements for puja and the vessels for use were stored in these. The box-like pathaayams were slightly bigger and were placed in the thekkini. These held grains specially exposed to the sun and the dew for preparing fried paddy.

Malar or fried paddy was made regularly since this held pride of place in puja offerings. M.T. Vasudevan Nair's stories have many references to the elders of the family seated on these pathayam boxes with a *chellapetti* holding their betel leaves and its accompaniments.

A pathaayam was not built, but only put together, because the thick planks of the sawn tree were merely fitted together. Paddy would lose its quality if it touched either the wall or the floor. So the pathaayam had wood on all sides and the panels in front were easily removable. In central Kerala, these were made from the wood of the jackfruit tree

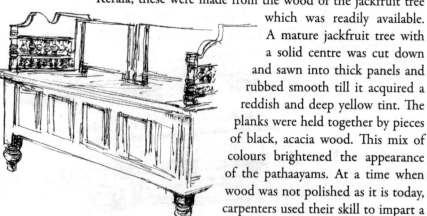

which was readily available. A mature jackfruit tree with a solid centre was cut down and sawn into thick panels and rubbed smooth till it acquired a reddish and deep yellow tint. The planks were held together by pieces of black, acacia wood. This mix of colours brightened the appearance of the pathaayams. At a time when wood was not polished as it is today, carpenters used their skill to impart a mirror like finish to it. The wood of a large tree, *aanjili*, was also used alternatively in some places.

Putting a pathaayam together was a skilled job. Each plank had to fit neatly into its designated place. So the angles and the joints had to be fixed correctly without any gaps. Nails were not used. When the pathaayam was closed, it was airtight with no space for insects to find their way in. I have seen, though rarely, a lock fixed on the topmost plank built as a lid to shut the pathaayam.

The pathaayams were designated by their size and capacity to hold one or two thousand *paras* of paddy. These large ones were placed in the pathaayappura. The paddy reaped in fields cultivated by the family and by those of the tenant farmers was stored here. The tenants measured out the paddy on the paved courtyard and the irikkanammas and the servants rushed around to transfer it to the pathaayams. One person sat on a bench outside the pathaayam while another got ready to press the grain down with his feet inside the pathaayam. This arrangement was made outside each pathaayam. It was the duty of the irikkanammas to carry head-loads of baskets filled with paddy to the pathaayam. Some of them made special conditions like insisting on a particular person taking their paddy from them. This led to some quarrels and unpleasantness. Even though we did not understand much, we were present to watch these romantic interludes. The air filled with paddy and dust caused itching, burning, and other allergies in us, but we watched anyway, fascinated by the excitement of this process.

There was a belief that objects brought by carpenters and braziers were not to be rejected which may have been the reason we had more vessels made of bell metal, brass, bronze, and wood than we needed. A pathaayam left carelessly half open above the western part of the building held such vessels, heaped together and never used. The green coating of mould on these things emitted a particular odour as we went past them. There was another riveting sight in this place with cockroaches crawling over the vessels. At the approach of any festival, the antharjanams would dip their jewellery in melted jaggery, spread them on clean cloth and leave it inside this pathaayam. In a day the cockroaches would have polished them, licking clean the intricate workings and spaces in the jewellery where dirt, sweat, and grease had accumulated. The jewellery would sparkle once again.

The pathaayams that were preserved most carefully were the ones that held the paddy seeds. There was a row of small pathaayams holding different seeds with the names of the genus written on the planks. There were seeds called virippu and mundakan which could be reaped twice a year as also *aryan, kattamodan, thavalakannan, chitteni,* and *cheera.* We also preserved with care the seeds our neighbours gave us for safekeeping. It seems they were afraid that hunger would force them to use these grains to cook their food and requested the large illams nearby to provide this security service. The sackfuls of grain brought from several houses were marked separately for identification and preserved carefully. It was considered bad luck if they did not sprout. Whole grains of paddy were winnowed two or three times and exposed to the sun and dew before being stored as seeds. They were spread to be aired and dried in the open courtyard and dispersed evenly twice a day using the feet. Some lines and squares were drawn on them to detect if any of it went missing from the spread. A guard was posted to prevent birds and dogs from eating the seeds.

Bunches of bananas were cut down and put out in the sun to dry the latex that flowed out, before being moved to their designated pathaayams. A slightly old single pathaayam was used for this. After storing the banana bunches, smouldering coal heaped on dry coconut fibre was placed inside and the door shut. The smoke would spread evenly inside and after three days of such exposure to the smoke, the bananas would ripen quickly and taste good. The smoke turned them golden yellow and never black.

I have not seen rice stored in pathaayams that stocked paddy. Sometimes rice was kept in pathaayam boxes and box-like pathaayams. Perhaps because people were readily available to pound the paddy, rice was usually filled in sacks and placed in a row on a bench in the pathaayam room.

In those days, there were also other ways of storing food. One such was called a *nilavara,* an underground cell in the house. This was a small room built six feet below the floor level, with steps leading down. Though they were mostly found under the staircase, they could be built anywhere in the nalukettu. This had a granite floor as well as granite walls and a granite ceiling. There would usually be a pathaayam above it. There were wooden bars near the door to allow for some ventilation. Pickles and preserves made of whole, tender, and cut mangoes, salted and dried mangoes, as well as other sorts were stored in the nilavara. Vinegar and oil were not used to preserve them. Since the room did not get any sunlight, no smell emanated from it to attract small insects and, therefore, the pickles remained intact for nearly a year.

It was very important to preserve the pickles. Only a senior member of the family was allowed to open and close the pickle jars. Whole mangoes both salted and spiced were placed in large jars. When mangoes were plentiful, the first of the pickles to be made was *kadumanga*, of tender mangoes. As the mangoes grew bigger, they were soaked in brine. The jars held one to two thousand mangoes. The mangoes were washed and cleaned, a hundred of them set apart and boiled and cooled salted water added to them. Then a hundred more mangoes were added and so on and so forth. When I came to Nilayamgode after my wedding, my mother-in-law would carry a lamp with a long handle, a coconut-shell ladle, a wooden vessel also with a handle, and go to this nilavara at supper time. She did not permit anybody else to do this. Her insistence on cleanliness was well known. She'd open the jars, take the mangoes out, and shut them carefully. I loved the coolness and the smells of this room and so sometimes I'd follow her carrying the lamp. These salted mangoes were washed clean before serving. *Athaazham*—supper— consisted of hot rice, a curry made with spices like pepper, fried pieces of dry bitter gourd, and salted mangoes. This meal was so good that we looked forward to it. When vegetables like bitter gourd and long beans grew in plenty, they as well as green chillies were salted, dried, and preserved in the same room.

In addition to the pathaayam and the nilavara, there were other repositories where food stuff was stored. In Nilayamgode, there was a pantry adjoining the kitchen where large Chinese jars were placed in a row. These were black and smooth with a wide middle and narrow ends. Today, they are shown off in living rooms as signs of a glorious past. But in my youth, they simply served as containers to store food stuff. If the jar was very tall, most of it appeared buried below the floor level. They were used in Nilayamgode to store salt, coconut oil, and tamarind. They could hold ten *para*s of salt, ten tins of coconut oil, ten *thulan* tamarind, and so on. A long handled ladle, *thavi*, was used as a salt-scoop and to measure out the oil. These jars were closed with wooden lids and covered with cloth tied around them. The jar containing tamarind would be above the floor level. The tamarind was de-seeded and pounded together with salt before storing it. The longer it stayed in the jar the more it lost its sharpness. To make *puliyinchi*, it was deemed absolutely necessary to use old tamarind that had turned black.

When the jars became empty, they were cleaned by lowering a little girl seven or eight years of age into them. Her hands and feet were cleaned before being sent down. She would clean the jars with coconut fibre, powdered acacia and water, and dry them. She would then be helped up and another lowered into the jar to dry the inside two or three times with a clean cloth. Children were very excited at the prospect of being lowered into the jars and waited for their turn impatiently. After all, this work was both unusual and out of the ordinary.

Pathaayams which stored paddy were considered by family members to be the inner sanctums of prosperity. Every new year, as a part of the first observances, these were worshipped alongside ears of corn. Their exterior was wiped clean of dust and cobwebs and decorated with batter made of powdered rice. They were festooned with the twigs and leaves of the jackfruit, the mango, and the gooseberry trees. The first ears of grain reaped by the master of the household himself were placed here after a puja. The mistress of the house welcomed this cluster of paddy with a lighted lamp and eight auspicious objects on a tray, to the accompaniment of verses recited to invoke divine blessing on the prosperity of their farms. At the same time, family members would chant: 'Fill, fill ... with heaped corn, fill the illam ... fill the baskets, fill the pathaayams, fill your stomachs ...' in loud tones.

Later, too, at every change of season, pathaayams were worshipped with special rites. Three days before the month of Kumbham, green bamboo leaves were placed together to shut the pathayam tight, a ceremony referred to as 'ucharal adakkal' when Aaran reaching its zenith. Aaran is another name for Mars. On the twenty-eighth day of the month of Makaram it was believed that the earth was in her menstrual period. All work was stopped on the fields on that day. Ploughing or raking the field was forbidden. For three days, all dealings in paddy were held in abeyance. Farmers rested at home since the earth was not to be disturbed in any way during that period. After three days, the pathaayams were opened before being shut once again. From the next day, it was work as usual. Several temples dedicated to Bhagawathi celebrated 'ucharal vela' to mark this period.

Similarly, in the month of Dhanu there was a ceremony called '*puli*'. From the twenty-eighth day of Dhanu to the third Makaram, the atmosphere was said to be contaminated by a poisonous vapour polluting the air. During that period, the pathaayams holding paddy seeds were secured tight and not opened even if the requirements of food made it imperative. Any laxity could affect the yield of a whole year. Therefore, people clung to these beliefs out of fear of the future.

Pathaayams were either a dream come true or a nightmare for the antharjanams. In their anxiety to secure the future of their daughters, they prayed that the girls would never starve. They petitioned Perumthrikko-vilappan and Annapoorneswari daily not only for the long married life of a daughter but also for them to have enough to eat all their lives. They repeatedly recited a mantra beseeching Lord Shiva to alleviate poverty and sorrow. Those who had daughters looked forward to giving them in marriage to families that could feed them throughout the year. They also longed to hear about the prosperity indicated by the pathaayams in their daughters' houses. If the paddy obtained from their tenant farmers was inadequate, their condition would be pitiable. The Namboodiris could either eat at the *vaara sadya* or go and live in rich households where they would be fed at large feasts. They did not feel the need to enquire about how their wives and children fared at home. There were many such people indifferent to the plight of their families. Therefore, when a wedding was arranged, the mothers would enquire whether there was enough paddy available in the illam. Nobody cared much to enquire whether the bride-groom was old, physically disabled, or mentally deficient. So, most of us made mental notes of the state of the pathaayams in other illams.

During the Second World War, scarcity of food was felt everywhere. Large imports of rice from Burma ceased. Kerala had never been self-sufficient in food and it was the rice grown from the *pokkali* paddy imported from Burma that had filled our granaries. This method of cultivation was relatively less expensive and was tried later at the *kolpadam* in Mookkuthala. When the fields were dry, the soil was raked and the seeds sown. By the time they sprouted, water would begin to fill the fields. The seedlings would rise along with the water level and be visible above it. The pokkali seed was a genus that assured a plentiful harvest. When it ripened, farmers would go out in a boat and harvest the paddy. With the kolpadams overflowing with water, it was difficult for anyone to distinguish the boundaries of their fields but they were satisfied with a rough calculation of the areas. So plentiful was the harvest that even if the people in passing boats gathered some paddy, no objection was made. But the rice cooked from that paddy lacked taste, which was perhaps why people discontinued its cultivation. This rice used to arrive plentifully in the Cochin harbour. Since it was grown under water, it never dried fully even in the sun. Sackfuls of this rice reached the harbour a few days after it was packed, by which time it would have begun to emit a certain odour. When it boiled, the smell intensified. It was very unpleasant to eat this 'sack-rice'. If their daughters had to be wed into a family where such rice was cooked, mothers would shed tears of anguish. But at least this rice was available in plenty at that time, whereas the famine that followed the World War was pitiable.

With no rice from Burma, the price of paddy went up steeply. Landlords started hoarding paddy in their pathaayams and selling it at high prices. That was when the levy came into effect. Calculations were made on the basis of the total members of the family and some few servants who were allotted six ounces of rice per meal till the next harvest. Paddy, over and above this requirement, was taken away by the government in their lorries. Paddy required for small feasts during celebrations was sanctioned separately. The calculations included the yield of one's own farming as well as tenant farming. That was the time when it could be said that the kitchens turned dark. This was the only topic of conversation at the temple tanks and temples. Vaarams and the feasts that followed were celebrated on a reduced scale. The antharjanams sighed in the kitchen as the Namboodiris paced angrily at the entrance. At weddings and obsequies, the numbers were limited to fifty with the supply officer's permission.

This problem did not seem to cause similar ripples in the kitchens of other communities. They started using tapioca, wheat, semolina, and other such edible things. It is said that an irikkanamma of Pakaravoor, Ammupennu, beat her breast and cried out aloud when macaroni was served to her on a leaf.

Our irikkanammas were greatly affected by this change. Used to getting vessels filled with food and seeing it as their right even after the family had eaten, they were now agitated to find empty vessels. They started cursing those who came to levy the paddy. Lakshmi would refer to them as the beggars. She took her anger out on them by adding a lot of chaff to the paddy when the officer was not looking.

Most of the supply officers were Iyers who knew that food was cooked in large quantities in Namboodiri illams since they, too, participated in the celebrations at temples and in illams. Therefore, when they measured out the paddy for levy they pretended not to notice the heaps of grain lying in the corners of the pathaayam. Antharjanams looked on such officers as the very god, Annapoorneswaran.

There also began the practice of selfishly hiding the paddy soon after the harvest. That was when we first heard about hoarding and black marketing. But we also heard that the paddy being transported illegally at night was confiscated by social workers and sold to the people at a low price. Late at night when lorries rushed past at breakneck speed, horns silent, we concluded that those were black marketeers at work.

At that time, I was in Nilayamgode. We struggled to divide the available food equally among all the members. My husband's ettan who was the kaaranavar of the family made sure that the women had enough to eat before he himself sat down to his meal.

That was how a new pathaayam came to be constructed at Nilayamgode. This was placed at the far end of the vadakkini adjoining the western side and could hold about thirty paras of rice. An ordinary wall-cupboard with two doors and four shelves was built above this space on the eastern wall of the vadakkini, the northern room, to store herbal medicines and concoctions. The shelves inside were loose and could be removed. When these were unhinged and the wooden back taken out, it was possible to enter the pathaayam. Soon after the harvest, the paddy was pounded and the rice was stored here. Food inspectors came to search the whole house but the pathaayam was not discovered. None of us felt guilty about this hoarding. We justified our actions by saying that after all there were children in the illam and this rice would come in handy when we absolutely needed it.

After independence, rationing was introduced. But the shortage of rice continued till the public distribution system was well in place.

I still remember a poem I had read in the monthly *Sanjayan* at the time of the food shortage. This was a take-off on a poem by Vallathol called '*Arippiraavu*'. The poem which began with apologies to the great poet had changed a line which read:

'The morning is a blessing to me' to 'The morning is a zero to me'. The parody went on as follows:

I'll not strew the rice,
Don't you understand
Our rationing system!
Yes, you are a guest
In my house;
But I, I am
A starving host.

Land reforms were among the most revolutionary changes in Kerala. Tenants became landlords and with the shrinking of property, the condition of the pathaayams also became pitiable. They were often empty. Namboodiri men started marrying women from their own community and the number of bedrooms in illams had proved inadequate. Pathaayams were dismantled and bedrooms made in their place. There was a good price to be got for pathaayam wood: it was so superior.

Later, these bedrooms, too, were deserted. The large joint family broke up and scattered to form nuclear families. The homes seemed orphaned and were dismantled and sold. The superior wood used in the pathaayams was now converted into the windows and doors of new houses. Recently when I went to Thiruvananthapuram, I had occasion to visit Abhayagramam which was Sugathakumari teacher's base for social work. There she had reconstructed, in its original design, an illam which she had received as a reward for her services. This had a pathaayam to hold paddy inside the machu in the nalukettu. When observed from the outer verandas, the four wooden sides of the pathaayam were seen to be the walls of the machu. It had a small hole which you could reach when you raised your arm. When you inserted a coin in it you would hear the sound of it falling—a '*chill*'—in a short time. Only after the pathaayam was emptied of all the paddy could the base planks be removed to take the coins out. The rationale must have been that they could use these coins to buy food when all the paddy in the pathaayam was exhausted.

Occasionally in homes that are still standing, it may be possible to see a pathaayam which could not be dismantled because it was an integral part of the building. But future generations may need to consult a dictionary to search for the meaning of the word 'pathaayam'.

27 Social Activism

I was a girl of fifteen when I was led to Nilayamgode, my husband's house.

Until then, I knew little about the world outside; had no contact with public life either. But the atmosphere at Nilayamgode, with its liberal views, encouraged me to participate in social activities. For three to four years, from the time of my wedding to about 1948, I worked with Antharjana Samajam, an organization formed under the Yoga Kshema Sabha, and became its secretary for a year when Parvathy Nenminimangalam was its president. By 1943, the Yoga Kshema Sabha activities had lost their former momentum and weakened slightly. One reason for the decline was that its prominent leaders had moved beyond community-oriented reforms and joined the Communist movement.

At around this time, an event of some importance took place at Ongallur near Nilayamgode—the wedding of an elderly Namboodiri. An old Namboodiri, his wife, their son, and the son's newly-wedded fourteen-year-old bride lived in an illam at Ongallur near Pattambi. One day quite suddenly, the son died, leaving the illam heirless. So the old Namboodiri decided to re-marry and have a son to perpetuate the family line.

The news of a seventy-year-old man's second wedding—while his fourteen-year-old daughter-in-law remained a widow at home—reached

---

* Translated by Radhika P. Menon

the Yoga Kshema Sabha. As preventing old-age-weddings was one of its activities, some members decided to picket the ceremony. The wedding was to take place at the bride's house. Many antharjanams and Namboodiris went to Ongallur to prevent it. Our leader was Arya Pallom and that was my first involvement in a public function.

As soon as we reached the bride's residence, their servants stopped us at the gate. So we surrounded the outer fence to block the ageing bridegroom and shouted: 'Can't you see a child widow's grief? Give *her* away in marriage. How can you think of a re-marriage when a fourteen-year-old remains widowed at home? This wedding should not take place'. Despite our great enthusiasm, our picketing failed. Spotting a corner we had not covered, some Namboodiris had lifted the old man over the fence and deposited him in the compound. Nobody noticed it and the wedding ceremony was performed with the priests whispering the mantras. Only when the sounds of joyous ululation, marking its conclusion, echoed and drowned our slogan shouts did we realize that our attempts had come to naught. We returned home, disappointed. Thus, the first public function I participated in was futile.

That incident took place towards the end of 1944. Not long afterwards, in 1945, the noted Ongallur meeting was held. It was here that E.M.S. Namboodiripad made the famous declaration, 'Let's make the Namboodiri a human being'. This helped energize the Yoga Kshema Sabha for the next couple of years. Many women took part in the Ongallur Convention—far more than in any previous one. In course of time, an organization called Antharjana Samajam was founded and I became its member and activist. Men contributed enormously towards forming it. Its aim was to spread awareness among antharjanams about the importance of education and employment. Once every two months, the Samajam members assembled at an illam. We usually reached there by ten or eleven in the morning and had lunch with the family. After that, we settled down in the southern wing of the nalukettu for the meeting. Most women-inmates of the illam joined us. A few old antharjanams, however, who believed it wrong to join such organizations kept away. They sat in the northern or eastern rooms, peering at us through barred windows. Every meeting began with the question, 'Should we let our children suffer our fate?' Then we elaborated our point. 'We have neither education nor knowledge; no idea about the outside world either. We are born and we die in the dark interiors of our nalukettu. Having no jobs, we have to beg for money. To get jobs, we should be educated. So let us educate our children and equip them for employment'—this was what we said. The menfolk too, sitting outside, listened to our talk.

Parvathy Nenminimangalam had a rare ability to present these ideas clearly and discretely. Called '*Chechi*' by all, she was more than twenty years my senior. She was slim and tall and very soft-spoken. She never spoke harshly or unpleasantly to anyone.

Arya Pallom was entirely different from Chechi in both looks and temperament. She spoke long and loud and if occasion demanded even aggressively. Arya Chechi had no inhibitions about speaking plainly even to Namboodiris. She was beautiful, fair-skinned, small built, and wore her hair short. Mr Pallom, her husband, was a Communist Party activist.

Arya Pallom was a nightmare to those Namboodiris who took pleasure in tugging at and bruising their wives' elongated earlobes or throwing *aavanipalaka*s at them and breaking their legs. Once, she severely scolded a housewife who spat at antharjanams for discarding their traditional

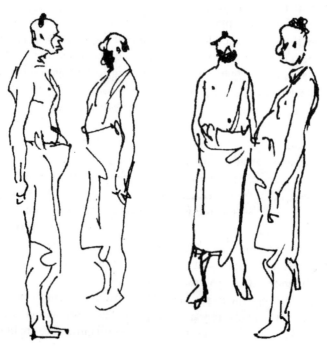

clothes and choosing to wear saris and blouses. Later, whenever that woman saw Arya Chechi, she hid behind her parasol and scampered away. In the meantime, some orthodox Namboodiris started lampooning Antharjana Samajam members.

They composed satirical poems about Arya Pallom and Parvathy Nenminimangalam and recited them publicly. The one on Parvathy Chechi, which was relatively harmless, began like this:

Parvathy Mangalam is here
She who discarded the palm-leaf umbrella.
Let's stay back
We may get to hear her speech
Perhaps.

But the poem on Arya Pallom was venomous as it made derogatory remarks about her husband:

Here comes Arya Pallom
Make way for her, everyone.
Behind her is Mr Pallom
Carrying a big box
And panting.
A slave to his wife.
Alas! What a state!
May the Almighty
Not curse anyone
With such a fate!

But Arya Chechi paid no heed to such cheap slanders. She had a rare combination of qualities—tremendous commanding power and an ability to love others selflessly. I used to go to Pallom Illam situated near Pattambi and even stayed there occasionally. Chechi's daughter, Devaki Warrier, and I were of the same age and also close friends. Before her death, Devaki wished to see me but unfortunately I could not make the trip. I remember the many happy days I spent with Arya Chechi and Devaki Warrier at Pallom.

Many young women wanted to attend the Antharjana Samajam meetings but very often the older members at the illam stood in their way. Arya Chechi took great pains to bring such women to the meetings. And if she ever came to know that they suffered hardships at home, she did not hesitate to take them under her wing. Once, my Edathi's daughter Kanjiramkode Unnikkali Antharjanam, inspired by Arya Chechi, attended a meeting. But when she returned to her in-laws' house, her husband's mother and his aunt declared harshly, 'Muslim women like you should not enter this house'. She could not step into the nalukettu or use the pond of the illam. Unnikkali's fate was terrible—she had to bathe in the temple pond and live in the outhouse. Her husband had no say in the matter. It was some time then that Unnikkali had a baby and there was no one to look after her. As soon as Arya Chechi heard of this, she stepped in and took care of her, like a mother.

The next meeting after the Ongallur Convention was held at Sukapuram. Although it was primarily an antharjanams' meeting, there were many men among the audience, V.T. Bhattathirippad being the most prominent among them. My sister-in-law, Parvathy Nilayamgode, who presided over it, said: 'Dear sisters, we have laid waste our lives. We have had bitter experiences and have done nothing with our lives. But we must save our children at least, by giving them education and helping them find employment.'

Suddenly, a woman from the audience sprang up and said, 'It is high time we threw away the black and dirty saligramas from our puja rooms. We don't need gods who cannot put an end to our miseries.' Then, pointing to V.T. Bhattathirippad, she concluded, 'Let us worship this saligrama instead.'

In response, V.T. stood up and rubbing his head, said with a smile, 'True. I am as black and smooth as a saligrama. But if you women want to be free of fetters, remember, only you can save yourselves. There is no point in worshipping me or anyone else.'

The Ottappalam meeting was presided over by Parvathy Nenminimangalam. When Parvathy Chechi was president of Antharjana Samajam and I, its secretary, one of our activities was to conduct an awareness campaign in illams in certain parts of Kerala. Three of us— Parvathy Chechi, Olappamanna Uma Antharjanam, and I—travelling mostly by bus and occasionally by car, covered most of the present-day Malappuram district and went right up to Kottayam. All this took nearly a month. Every day we chose an illam and stayed there for a day. We talked to the inmates about the need to educate children and explained why women should take up jobs and earn an independent living. Most of our hosts welcomed us warmly although at certain illams we did not even get past the gates.

Amma did not approve of my activities at all. Earlier she had never permitted us, her daughters, even to wrap a pleated mundu around ourselves or to part our hair to one side because she considered such styles, fast, fashionable, and therefore wrong. Once, she even made my elder sister-in-law write me a letter to convey her displeasure at my travels. However, by the time it reached me, I had already made all the preparations for the trip. But in the course of our journey, on my brothers' invitation, my friends and I stayed at Pakaravoor for a night. Anticipating our visit and perhaps wishing to avoid me, Amma had her dinner well before dusk and went to bed. I didn't get a chance to see or talk to her the next morning either. She remained in her room till we left. Though my heart was heavy, I could see that my companions were even more distressed than I.

Self-employment and steady income for women—these were the mantras we sought to instil in antharjanams wherever we went. Gradually, we felt a strong desire to put these ideas into practice. This, in turn, gave rise to the concept of starting a centre to train antharjanams who had neither any formal education nor previous work experience. With some training, we believed, they could take up small jobs at home and earn a modest income but the project needed big funding. During our travels, we received contributions from several illams and we decided to use the funds to set up a training centre. Finding a suitable place was the next problem. Luckily, a social worker and lover of art, Chiramangalam C.M.C. Namboodiripad and his son, the reformist and political activist Yagnamoorthy Namboodiripad vacated a large section of their *mana* at Lakkidi in Ottappalam and permitted us to use it without paying rent. V.T. Bhattathirippad inaugurated the training centre.

Antharjanams from several illams, numbering between forty and fifty, came and stayed together at the centre as a commune. They were taught the art of spinning, weaving cloth, and making paper envelopes. Everyone cooperated to prepare food and do the routine chores. I could not stay there permanently but made frequent visits and completed the training.

Some women at the centre later wrote and staged a play 'Thozhil Kendrathilekku' (To the Workplace), the first ever to be scripted, directed, and acted by antharjanams. Arya Pallom and two or three others prepared the script, picking the theme and dialogues from the numerous discussions and exchange of ideas that had taken place earlier. It was staged in 1948.

The Centre worked well for about nine months. By then, some antharjanams found it difficult to stay away from home for long spells. Their husbands and children were raising objections. Besides, a few orthodox Namboodiris had started a vilification campaign against the Centre. In his inauguration speech, V.T. Bhattathirippad had made references to Kuriyedathu Thaatri, stating that there was at least one Thaatri who pointed an accusing finger at patriarchal authority. Some reactionary Namboodiris used this idea to allege that the training centre was set up to create more Thaatris.

The centre had withstood such vile calumnies for some time and even staged a good play. But gradually the number of antharjanams dwindled and, by the end of 1948 or the beginning of 1949, the centre had to be closed down. The founding and closure of the training centre formed the last stage of reform movement within the Namboodiri community. It was also a period of activism that succeeded in bringing mere homemakers like me to the forefront of public life.

28 No Regrets

After 1950, the activities of the Yoga Kshema Sabha came to an end. Following the partition of our ancestral property at Nilayamgode in Chathanoor, my husband, our children, and I shifted to a new house at Thichoor. The old joint family thus disintegrated and a nuclear family took shape. Although I never went to school, my children did.

This change was not confined to Nilayamgode. Almost all Namboodiri families underwent a similar transformation. Joint families broke up giving way to smaller units and parents sent their children to school. The educated children moved on, motivated by a desire to work, earn, and have an independent means of livelihood. As the environment visualized by the Namboodiri reformers emerged, the reform movement naturally and slowly receded.

On looking back, I find little similarity between my present-day life and the childhood I spent in my old illam. How much and how fast things have changed in fifty-sixty years! I can emphatically state that life today is better than ever before.

Today, there is no sorrow specific to a Namboodiri family. It has the same joys and sorrows, the same anxieties and ambitions as any other family. Time, the great leveller, has ironed out most differences.

* Translated by Radhika P. Menon

Here, my brief autobiographical account comes to a close. The reason for it is obvious and simple—after this, there can be no autobiography which claims to be the first by an antharjanams or exclusively about us.

Glossary

aavanipalaka	:	an oval-shaped plank used as a seat during rituals or religious ceremonies
Aayilyam	:	the ninth lunar asterism
aayirakudamaaduga	:	a treatment that involves pouring a thousand pots of water continuously on the patient's head
achan	:	father
ada	:	a kind of rice flour cake, made of jaggery and shredded coconut
Agni devata	:	the God of Fire
akathullal	:	literally, the woman inside the house. In this case an antharjanam, a Namboodiri woman
Ambalavasis	:	a group of communities who by tradition provide various services in the temple
amma	:	mother
ammamma	:	mother's mother
ammathu	:	mother's ancestral home
ana	:	a coin in India, used during the British rule; 1/16th of a rupee

Anand	:	here, Vishwanathan Anand, international chess champion and Grand Master
Anandamath	:	famous Bengali novel (1882), by Bankim Chandra Chattopadhyay
antharjanam	:	a Namboodiri woman (the word literally means the person indoors)
'Anupama Kripanidhi'	:	the opening words of *Karuna*, a poem by the famous poet, Kumaran Asan
apphan	:	father's younger brother (among Namboodiris)
appam	:	a savoury made of fermented rice flour
Atham	:	the thirteenth lunar asterism
Attumanamel	:	name of the ancestral house of Unniarcha, a well-known heroine of 'Vadakkan Paatukal'
aval kuzhachathu	:	a dish made of flattened rice and jaggery
Azhakiya Ravanan	:	name of Ravana, elaborately and regally dressed to attract Sita in the Ashoka garden
beedi	:	a country cigarette
Bhagavatam	:	a Hindu Purana, its primary focus is the process of bhakti yoga (personal devotion to the Supreme Lord) in which Mahavishnu or Krishna is considered the Supreme, all-embracing god of all Gods.
Bhagavatha Saptaham	:	a seven-day recital of *Bhagavatham*, one of the eighteenth Puranas sacred to Lord Mahavishnu
Bhagavati	:	Devi, the presiding Goddess of the temple at Mookkuthala
Bhangi	:	the lowest in the caste system of north India—one who cleans toilets and, in earlier times, physically removed human waste
bindi	:	originally, a dot or mark made at a point between the eyebrows to protect the portion considered

to be the sixth chakra or the seat of 'concealed wisdom'. According to followers of Tantrism, this chakra is the exit point for kundalini energy. The bindi is said to retain energy and strengthen concentration. Today it is generally regarded merely as a decorative mark

Brahminiamma : the wife of a Nambisan, a superior class of temple servants

chamata : a fire-ritual using twigs of the chamata (*Butea Frondosa* a.k.a. flame of the forest)

Changanpuzha : Changanpuzha Krishna Pillai (1911–1948) well-known Malayalam poet

chechi : elder sister

Cherumi : a woman from a caste that was considered 'untouchable'

'*Chintavishtayaya Sita*' : 'Contemplative Sita' (1920), considered one of Kumaran Asan's masterpieces. A philosophical poem (monologue) in which Sita, abandoned by Lord Rama, bewails her lot, bursts into righteous indignation, and finally accepts her fate

chottara : room used by women-attendants to store their share of lunch. The word is derived from 'choru' or cooked rice; 'ara' means 'room'

companions : Nair women who were a cut above the servant class, to be distinguished from the above category who were attendants

C.V. Raman Pillai : (1858–1922) One of the most noted of early Malayalam novelists

Dakshinamoorthy : one of the names of a form of Lord Shiva meaning 'the Lord of the South', from the belief that a youthful Shiva sat facing southwards and instructed elderly sages

Damayanthi : in the story 'Nala Charitham', King Nala, in disguise, wooed and won Damayanthi, the

		daughter of King Bhima of Vidarbha and later deserted her in the forest
dashapushpam	:	ten flowers or plants used as offerings in rituals, puja, etc.
deeksha	:	a period of penance
devas	:	minor deities
Devi puja	:	ceremonial rites performed for the goddess
Dhanu	:	the ninth month of the zodiac
dhaara	:	anointing with oil/milk/coconut water
Durgeshanandini	:	novel by Bankim Chandra Chattopadhyay (1865) which features a Rajput hero and a Bengali heroine
edathi	:	elder sister
Ekadashi	:	the eleventh day from the new moon or full moon
E.M.S. Namboodiripad	:	(1909–1998), an Indian Communist leader and the first Chief Minister of Kerala. He was associated with V.T. Bhattathiripad, M.B. Bhattathiripad, and other social reformers
erissery, pulissery, etc.	:	curries favoured by Keralites
ettan	:	elder brother
exchange marriage	:	a brother and sister from one family marrying a brother and sister from another
gurudakshina	:	the gift offered by the pupil to his teacher at the end of his/her education
gurukulam	:	the living quarters of a teacher where pupils stay during the period of education
Guruvayoorappan	:	Lord Vishnu, who is worshipped in the famous temple at Guruvayoor in Kerala
Harishchandra	:	in Hindu mythology, a king who always told the truth

Harishri Ganapathaye Namah	:	part of a shloka invoking blessings from Lord Ganapathi, writing which a child is initiated into learning
helpers	:	Nair women from poor families who worked as servants in Namboodiri Illams
homam	:	sacrificial fire
Idavam	:	the tenth month of the Malayalam calendar
ilanjikkuru	:	seed of the *Mimusops Elengi* a.k.a. kabiki, baula, or Spanish cherry
illam	:	the house of a Namboodiri
Indulekha	:	the first Malayalam novel by O. Chandu Menon, (1847–1899) published in 1889. It was written to explain and critique the cultural practices of sambandham and marumakkatayam, that prevailed among Nairs
Jnanapana	:	'Song of Divine Wisdom' composed by Poonthanam Namboodiri (1547–1640). It imparts transcendental knowledge by describing man's experiences in the world
kaalan	:	a gravy made with curds and coconut
kadukka	:	gall-nut
Kaikottikali	:	a type of dance in which women in typical Kerala costume stand in a circle round the traditional lamp and move to a set pattern of steps and clapping of hands
kaitha	:	pandanus tree
kaithapoo	:	pandanus flower
kallukali, vattukali	:	games played with marbles/smooth stones
kanmashi	:	kohl, eyeliner
Kanni	:	the second month of the Malayalam calendar
karanavar	:	the head of an extended family

Karkidakam	:	July-August in the Malayalam month
karuka	:	a kind of grass used for rituals
Karuna	:	one of Kumaran Asan's major poems (1923) based on Buddhist legends. It re-tells the story of a courtesan, Vasavadatta, who attains salvation through repentance
kashali, poothali	:	various traditional patterns of necklaces
K.B. Sreedevi	:	(b. 1940) a Malayalam novelist whose works are exclusively about Namboodiri society
Keechaka	:	an evil character in the Mahabharata who is killed by Bhima, the Pandava. He is the villain in the popular Kathakali episode 'Keechaka Vadham'
Keshava Dev	:	(1904–1983) a famous novelist whose works conveyed his sympathies with the oppressed classes
Khilafat	:	a revolutionary Islamic movement against the British during India's freedom struggle
kolpadam	:	fields on land reclaimed from the backwaters
koombala	:	a tender layer of the arecanut spathe
K.P.S. Menon	:	K.P. Shankunni Menon (1896–1982) was a member of the Central Sangeeta Nataka Academy
kudiveppu	:	a ritual celebrating the bride's first entry to the groom's residence
Kumaran Asan	:	(1873–1924) considered the foremost of the poetic trinity of Malayalam. His poem 'Veenapoovu' ('The Fallen Flower' 1908) launched a decisive break from traditionalism
Kummi, Kurathi, Vanchipattu, Anchadipattu, Porvilipattu	:	songs sung on specific occasions like a group dance, gypsy dance, boat races, battle challenges, etc.
Kuttikkave	:	a way of addressing a Namboodiri girl

Lakshmi	:	Lord Vishnu's consort, the goddess of wealth
Lord Ganesha	:	Ganapathi, the son of Lord Shiva and Goddess Parvathy
machu	:	a wooden enclosure specially constructed on the western wing of a nalukettu to house the paradevatha, ancestral spirits, and other valuables including items of food
madhom	:	a brahmin's house
mana	:	the house of a Namboodiri
manchal	:	a box-carriage drawn by men
Manipravalam	:	a style of poetry, using a mixture of Sanskrit and Malayalam words. 'mani' in Malayalam means 'ruby' and 'pravalam' in Sanskrit is 'coral'. This particular school of poetry was patronized by the upper classes, especially the Namboodiris
mezhukku puratti	:	a dish of vegetables cooked in coconut oil till they turn golden brown; literally, mezhukku: oil; purati: smeared
mukkaal	:	three-fourths of 'chakram', a coin that was in currency in Old Travancore
mundakan	:	a type of paddy sown in the month of September-October
mundu	:	an ankle-length piece of unstitched cloth wrapped around and tucked in at the waist
murukku	:	a savoury made of rice and gram flour and deep fried
nadumuttam	:	inner courtyard
nalukettu	:	a quadrangular building with an inner courtyard, in the traditional Kerala architectural style
Nair	:	an upper caste among Hindus in Kerala
nalpamara	:	a fragrant herb

Nambiar	:	a sect among Nairs, usually temple servants (Ambalavasis)
Nambisan	:	a superior class of temple servants
Namashivaya	:	a prayer sung in praise of Lord Shiva
Namboodiri	:	upper class Brahmins of Kerala. They follow the concept of 'Sankaranarayanan' which combines the rituals of Shaivism and Vaishnavism
nataka shala	:	a building meant for staging plays and dances
nilaathu	:	a cauldron
onapudava	:	new clothes presented at Thiruvonam
oottuppuras	:	dining halls
othu	:	recitation of the Vedas
para	:	a measure used for paddy or rice
Parvathi	:	Lord Shiva's consort. Also worshipped as Bhagavathi
pathayappura	:	a building containing a barn. Its upper storey has large rooms that are generally used by Namboodiris and visiting Brahmins
pavithramothiram	:	a gold ring made in the fashion of the 'darbha' ring
payasam	:	pudding, made of milk, sugar or jaggery, and rice
puja	:	ceremonial worship
prathaman	:	a thick liquid sweet made of jackfruit or banana jam, or lentils with jaggery and coconut milk added to it
pula	:	after a death in the family, the fifteen day period of official mourning
pulinkari	:	a curry with tamarind juice as its chief ingredient
punja	:	wet cultivation of paddy which is harvested in March or April
Pulayi	:	a woman from the untouchable Pulaya caste

Puranas	:	holy scriptures
Rigvedis	:	Brahmins who profess and live according to the teachings of the Rig Veda
roja nuts	:	a brand name of betel nuts
saadhanam	:	literally, 'object'
sahridayas	:	people who appreciate literature and the arts
saligrama	:	a fossilized stone, sacred to Lord Vishnu (and hence worshipped), found in the river Gandaki.
samaavarthanam	:	a ritual that marks the completion of Vedic education
sambandham	:	informal marriage alliance among Namboodiris with girls belonging to lower castes, that is, from royal families as well as Nair, Warrier, Pisharadi, and other communities
sambhaaram	:	diluted buttermilk, salted and spiced with cumin seed and ginger
Saraswati	:	goddess of art and knowledge in Hindu mythology
Sarpathullal	:	an elaborate puja to the snake-god
Savitri	:	the wife of Satyavan who struggled with Yama, Death, and brought her husband back from the dead. Her story is narrated in the Hindu Purana, *Prathama Prathisruthi*
Sarojinikuttiyude Kadunkai, Kavalappara Komban	:	pulp fiction titles
shastris	:	men learned in the Hindu code of life and ethics
Shiva	:	the third member of the Hindu Trinity the great ascetic and the god of destruction.
Sheelavati	:	a popular song of the time which told the story of the eponymous heroine's wifely virtues; considered a must-read for unmarried Namboodiri girls

shloka	:	a verse in the epic metre consisting of two lines of sixteen syllables each
Shraavanam	:	the month of July-August when the full moon enters the asterism Shravana
Shudra	:	the lowest of the four castes among Hindus
Sivapuranam	:	one of the eighteen puranas, generally recited during Shiva puja and Durga puja
S.K. Pottekatt	:	(1913–1982) famous travelogue writer and novelist
smaarthan	:	inquisitor
smaarthavichaaram	:	religious trial of a Namboodiri woman by Brahmin priests when she is suspected of adultery
somayaga	:	a Vedic ritual, supposed to make a Namboodiri a complete Brahmin
Somayaji	:	a Brahmin who has performed the 'Somayaga'
Sri Krishna Charitham	:	Sri Krishna's story
Thakazhi	:	Thakazhi Sivasankara Pillai (1912–1999), a Malayalam novelist and short story writer who focused on the oppressed classes set against historic detail
thampuran	:	male member of a royal family, also term of respectful address to non-royal upper castes
tharavadu	:	ancestral house
thirumeni	:	respectful term of address
Thiruvathira	:	the sixth lunar asterism
Thiruvonam	:	the twenty-second lunar asterism. Harvest festival in Kerala, celebrated for a week culminating on the day Thiruvonam star falls in the month of Chingam in the Malayalam calendar, August/September in the English
thorthu	:	a thin cotton towel

Thulam	:	October-November in the English calendar
tilak	:	same as 'bindi'
uduthu thudangal	:	formal ceremony marking a girl's entry into womanhood, during which she is made to wear a cotton loincloth
Ulloor	:	Ulloor Parameswara Iyer (1877–1949), considered the second of the grand poetic trinity of the twentieth century renaissance in Malayalam literature
Umakeralam	:	an epic composed by Ulloor Parameswara Iyer in 1914. It revolves around some significant episodes in the history of the royal family of Travancore in the seventeenth century
umikkeri	:	burnt husk of paddy
Unniarcha	:	well-known heroine in Vadakku Pattukal, the Northern ballads, distinguished by her valour and martial skills
the body placed on the floor	:	is a common practice among Hindus to symbolize the body's final return to Bhoomi Devi, Mother Earth
Upanayanam	:	a ritual symbolizing the progress of an upper caste boy's entry into a life bound by the shastras/truth/ vedic way of life
uri	:	a grip made of rope suspended from the ceiling.
uruli	:	a shallow vessel made of bell metal
Uthradam	:	the twenty-first lunar asterism; the star before Thiruvonam
vaaka	:	the flowering tree, acacia
Vaakya	:	*Vaakya Vritti* by Adi Shankaracharya (788–820 CE), which gives an exhaustive explanation of the Upanishadic Mahaavaakya 'That Thou Art' [Tat Twam Asi]
vaaram	:	a temple festival

vaara sadya	:	feast following the religious ritual of vaaram
vadakkanpattu/ vadakkangatha	:	songs of heroic exploits from North Malabar
vadakke ara	:	a room in the north of the house
vadakkupuram	:	northern side and hence the back of the house
vadikkini	:	northern part of an old style Kerala house—the nalukettu
vaidyan	:	an ayurvedic doctor
valiyamma	:	elder aunt
Vallathol	:	Vallathol Narayana Menon (1878–1958), the third of the poetic trinity of Malayalam
valiyettan	:	eldest brother
Veda Vyasa	:	the central and much revered figure in the majority of Hindu traditions. Author of the Mahabharata
virippu	:	cultivation in the month of September-October
Vishnu	:	the second member of the 'Thrimurtis' in Hindu mythology; He is the Preserver
vishukani	:	auspicious objects to be looked at first thing in the morning on Vishu day; supposed to bring good luck in the new year
V.T. Bhattathirippad	:	a social critic and reformer, well-known dramatist, and prominent freedom fighter, born in a village in Palakkad district, Kerala; worked to reform Namboodiri social customs aimed to demolish the barbaric practices of Namboodiri orthodoxy
vritham	:	number of beats in a verse
Warrier	:	a caste of temple servants (Ambalavasis) which makes garlands for the deity
yagam	:	holy sacrifice to propitiate the deities
yagagni	:	the sacrificial fire

Yoga Kshema Sabha	:	an organization formed in 1908 by progressive-minded Namboodiris. Initially it had broad objectives, with a major thrust on eradication of illiteracy and spread of modern education
zari	:	brocade of gold or silver